Opera manuū nostrarū dirige supra nos

Opus manuū nostrarū dirige

Serve God and be chearefull

✝ Heer John Hacket being raised to the Episcopate as 75⁰ Bishop of Lichfield, a.d. 1661, and finding this House of God overthrown by violent and wicked hands, to impelled by a holy desire to rebuild that which had been broken down through his own personal labours and munificence, as well as by the offerings of the faithful, he was enabled after a space of eight years, to rededicate it to the worship of Almighty God a.d. 1669 ✝

Giving thanks to God, for the pious example of Bishop Hacket, by which after generations of benefactors have been moved to carry on his work, towards the complete reparation of this Cathedral Church, a grateful diocese dedicates this window to his honoured memory on the Festival of S. Chad, a.d. 1901

THE
CATHEDRALS
OF BRITAIN

OVERLEAF *The repair of Lichfield Cathedral in the 1660s:*
a window of 1901 by C. E. Kemp and The Knocker used
to claim sanctuary in Durham Cathedral.

THE CATHEDRALS OF BRITAIN

David L. Edwards

MOREHOUSE PUBLISHING
WILTON, CONNECTICUT

First published in Great Britain 1989 by
Pitkin Pictorials Limited, North Way, Andover,
Hampshire SP10 5BE

First American edition published by
Morehouse Publishing, 78 Danbury Road,
Wilton, Connecticut 06897

**Library of Congress Cataloging-in-
Publication Data**
Edwards, David Lawrence.
    The cathedrals of Britain/David L. Edwards —
    1st American ed.   p. cm.
    Includes bibliographical references.
    ISBN 0–8192–1503–1
    1. Cathedrals – Great Britain – Themes,
    motives. I. Title.
NA5461.E44   1989
726′.6′0942–dc20   89–12740
                                         CIP

Designed by Crispin Goodall
Picture research by Ann Lockhart
Typeset in Great Britain by Anton Graphics Ltd,
Andover, Hampshire
Colour reproduction by The Scanning Gallery,
Tonbridge, Kent

Produced by Mandarin Offset
Printed and bound in Hong Kong

ISBN 0–8192–1503–1

*The Decorated tracery
of the east window of
Carlisle Cathedral
(about 1350).*

CONTENTS

Preface

PREFACE

When invited to write a book on Britain's cathedrals to be illustrated by the best of the publisher's unique collection of photographs, I felt that it would be a marvellous subject. I believe that everyone who has come within range of these amazing and humbling buildings will share my feeling. They were built to the glory of God but they certainly are part of the glorious heritage of Britain and the world. In England no buildings are more important as architecture or as embodiments of history, and not many buildings contain so much beauty. I was glad to be asked to include the cathedrals of Scotland and Wales and the Roman Catholic Church. To help anyone to understand why, how and when these buildings were raised and adorned – what a pleasant task! To describe the history and appearance of eighteen of the greatest cathedrals in a little more detail – what a fascinating challenge!

One reason why I am enthusiastic is because at 60 I have so many good memories. I was a schoolboy in the shadow of Canterbury Cathedral, at the King's School. I have often gone to services in Oxford's little cathedral and in the great chapel of King's College, Cambridge (which is cathedral-like), where I was Dean. I was a canon of Westminster Abbey (also cathedral-like) and Dean of the magnificent Norman cathedral in Norwich before moving back to London and to Southwark Cathedral, which is my present responsibility and love. But I have sufficient respect for these buildings which are triumphs of meticulous craftsmanship to know that enthusiasm about them ought not to degenerate into sentimental gush. I am grateful to the many experts whose books I have used and to the Deans and Librarians who have checked my drafts for accuracy. Above all I am grateful to my wife Sybil, who is so patient about my reading and writing and who in more than one sense accompanies me on my expeditions.

A technical term is explained when it is first used and is listed in the index. But I have tried to write for my fellow-amateurs.

D.L.E.

THE CATHEDRAL—WHY?

Christ in Majesty *by Sir Jacob Epstein dominates*
Llandaff Cathedral. The concrete arch and organ case
were designed by George Pace during the
reconstruction of the 1950s.

1 THREE HISTORIES

The Lady chapel of Llandaff, built about 1280.

Let us begin not with an abstract idea but with three of Britain's smaller cathedrals, because they are excellent examples of what a cathedral is.

A cathedral rests not on a theory but on earth. It is made of stone, brick, wood, glass, iron, brass, tile and paint – and it is built with intelligence and sweat. As many generations of architects and craftsmen have known, it requires many practical skills to construct it and to repair it. And as many generations of visitors know, it means many different things to many different people. Perhaps it means a landmark, giving the townscape unity and dignity. Perhaps it means a place where it is not raining. Perhaps it means a marvel of architecture. Perhaps it means a museum where you can feel that the past is real and near. Perhaps it means sacredness of a kind you do not want to define. To admire it, you do not have to be a religious believer. But a cathedral is also a creation imagined by the human spirit in order to affirm an aspiration and a faith, and as such it is used and valued every day. It assembles clergy and musicians (listen to the choir!), vergers and voluntary helpers (look at the flowers!), the faithful few and the occasional church-goers (enjoy the celebration!). It attracts a multitude of visitors if it is richly historic or (as in Coventry or Liverpool) of outstanding interest as a new building. About two million visitors a year go into the great churches of Canterbury and York and about half a million more into St Paul's. (Westminster Abbey gets about three million.) Some visitors become pilgrims. They find that this palatial house of God, useless when assessed from most angles, arouses awe and affection. It can stimulate a religious experience. At any time when one enters the Roman Catholic cathedral in Westminster (for example) people are praying.

Llandaff Cathedral

Let us go to Llandaff, where we find one of the four cathedrals of medieval Wales. Llandaff is still a village on the edge of fields but it is linked with Cardiff by Cathedral Road's homes of Victorian and Edwardian prosperity. Nowadays the most striking internal feature of the cathedral is a concrete arch, bearing in front of the organ case an aluminium figure of Christ by Sir Jacob Epstein. This Lord is both Jewish and universal, both tragic and triumphant. Pleading with sad eyes and outstretched arms, he stands high over the congregation and over a chequered history. This sculpture of the 1950s is one of the most eloquent statements in Britain of the message that all cathedrals try to impart.

The church lies in a hollow which was a sacred burial ground before Christianity came. Probably the site was chosen because here a priest could serve the people living on the coast in front of the hills but could remain hidden from any pirates. About AD 560, tradition says, Bishop Teilo established a *llan*, a very simple monastery, near the river Taff. He was one of the leading missionaries among the people called by the English (not then Christian) *wealas* or 'foreigners'. The Welsh Church maintained old-fashioned Celtic customs which were not thought proper in far-distant Rome but which suited a tribal society. For example, the Celtic bishop was a holy man rather than a lord, living simply and spreading grace by preaching and the Christian sacraments. In South Wales today almost 30 places or churches are still named after Teilo. In Llandaff the church which became a cathedral for his successors was little more than a cottage: its dimensions were recorded as 8.5 metres (28 feet) long, 4.5 metres (15 feet) wide and 6 metres (20 feet) high. All that remains from those early days is a stone cross, recovered from the wall of a shed in 1870, full of the entwined, unending lines which signified eternity. At once we are made aware of the first fact about any cathedral: big or small, it must contain the seat or throne (in Greek or Latin, *cathedra*) of a bishop. (So Westminster Abbey, for all its glory, is not a cathedral.) A second fact is that people like at least one bishop in a cathedral's history to have been a saint, someone scented with eternity.

Naturally when a Norman bishop was appointed to this outpost of Norman power (Urban, in 1107), he wanted a more impressive headquarters. Money was always a problem – all the more so since in his time most of the estates owned by the cathedral were transferred to endow churches in England – but eventually a complete new cathedral was dedicated in 1266. During that period architectural styles evolved. A large arch survives above the chief or 'high' altar; we can tell that it is 'Romanesque' (the European term) or 'Norman' (as the English call this style) because it is rounded like the arches built by the Romans. To this day it dominates the areas where the clergy and singers are placed during the services: the areas known as the 'presbytery' (*presbyter* is the Latin word from which 'priest' is derived) and 'choir', together called the 'chancel' because they are often behind a screen, for which the Latin is *cancellus*. ('Choir', a word which comes from the Greek or Latin *chorus*, is sometimes spelt 'quire' when it refers to this part of a building rather than to the singers, but in this book there ought to be no danger of confusion.) So we move towards the other end of the 'nave', the people's part of the church which is said to look like the inside of a ship (in Latin *navis*) and to be for the people the ark of salvation in life's stormy seas. There the arches change. They are now more pointed. They seem to be echoing the ancient phrase in Christian worship: '*Sursum corda!* Lift up your hearts!' Now we are made aware of another fact. It is thought fitting that a cathedral should be dignified as a piece of architecture, the best of the day – not only as a status symbol for the bishop but also as (in the biblical phrase) 'the gate of heaven'. In the Middle Ages most people lived in cottages which we might call hovels. But in the cathedral there was a 'vault' or ceiling lifted high above the things of earth.

If the whole of that medieval cathedral in Llandaff had survived, it would be impressive. But how much more impressive is the story of building and rebuilding since 1266! In the Middle Ages they wanted more light in the church, so they inserted larger windows. They wanted to honour Mary as the Mother of the Church as well as of the Saviour, so they built a Lady chapel. They wanted a strong tower, so Jasper Tudor, the uncle of Henry VII, gave one which has proved indestructible.

In the time of Henry VIII Protestantism took over, here tragically allied with English colonialism and vandalism. The period is known as the Reformation – but it deformed the country's beautiful churches. The senior clergy of Llandaff now cared little. Bishops were Englishmen who came and, as rapidly as possible, went. St Teilo's shrine was destroyed; Cromwell's soldiers pillaged; the choir was disbanded. Storms came and the south-west tower collapsed. Neglect continued and the roof fell in. John Wood, an architect who did incomparably better work when he began the transformation of Bath from medieval to Georgian, built a cheap church among the ruins, at a time when the Welsh people were

filling the spiritually-alive chapels of the Methodists and other nonconformists. Then the revival of Anglican pride and concern reached Wales and the Victorians, strengthened by new wealth from coal and iron, rebuilt the cathedral from end to end, once again with a south-west tower and spire, an organ and a choir school (the only one in Wales), and decent houses for enthusiastically resident clergy. John Prichard was their architect. Much of their work, however, was wrecked by a German land-mine in 1941 and reconstruction (with George Pace as architect) took another 17 years. Today Llandaff Cathedral serves a district or 'diocese' of the Church in Wales (the Anglicans), covering an area where a third of the Welsh population lives – and this battered building is more lovely and more loved than ever.

Ripon Cathedral

To see again how much history can be included in a small cathedral, let us go to Ripon amid the peaceful beauties of North Yorkshire.

Here we find a 'crypt' (basement) built about 670 by St Wilfrid. Its crude strength, originally protecting 'relics' or bones of saints, is a reminder of the courage of that missionary bishop, who was also an evangelist in Sussex, in an age of fierce wars between England's tribal kingdoms and fierce work to subdue the countryside to human needs. The rather larger crypt of another of St Wilfrid's churches survives at Hexham in Northumberland. Craftsmen brought over from continental Europe were used. The church above this Ripon crypt was destroyed by invading Danes but successive Archbishops of York rebuilt it as a centre for their visits to this part of their vast diocese. Other great churches, similarly used by the archbishops, survive in Beverley and, far to the south, in Southwell. The building which we see in Ripon is a patchwork since different archbishops had different, always fashionable, architectural tastes.

The chapter house where the clergy (called 'canons') meet dates from the end of the Norman or Romanesque period (approximately 1050-1200). In the north transept and in part of the nave there is still the Norman strength in the walls but the arches are becoming rather more pointed and the architecture is becoming 'Transitional'. Then we see the simplicity of the Early English style (1175-1250). This style is attractively exhibited on the west front, where the 'lancet' windows (so called because slender and pointed) are altogether lighter in spirit. The later, more ambitious, Decorated style (1250-1340) is called 'geometric' in its early development and 'curvilinear' later. Ripon provides a fine

example in the east window, as long as a cricket pitch, with ribs of stone ('tracery') intersecting in a geometric pattern.

Finally, we admire the Perpendicular style (1340-1530) in the reconstruction of the nave, which was begun after the fall of the central tower but never quite finished; the great arch at the east end of the nave is Perpendicular on one side only. In this style far less depends on the intricate work of the stone-carver. His skill tends to be concentrated on the elaborate stone ceiling, the arched 'vault'. Otherwise there is simple tracery in the windows and on the walls: although there are still some curves, the dominant pattern is made by the straight lines which go up and across. It is a style unique to English stonemasons. The last period of the Middle Ages was also a great time for English carpenters, as we can see in the canopied stalls for the clergy, carved with a tremendous energy of imagination and skill in the 1490s.

When the Archbishops of York were reduced in status at the Protestant Reformation, a church such as this lost much of its purpose, for Ripon has never been a large town. The spires which had given the three squat towers some height in the Middle Ages became unsafe, were removed and were never replaced. But in 1604 canons were appointed again, with a dean to chair them (a 'Dean and Chapter'). When in 1836 the population of this part of Yorkshire had grown so much that a separate diocese was needed, this ancient church of St Peter and St Wilfrid was available to serve as a cathedral. The next half-century saw much necessary restoration of the stonework and much adornment of the interior. The bronze and marble pulpit is a product of the 'Arts and Crafts' movement inspired by William Morris and flourishing at the time of its erection, 1913 – when no one expected the great war which is memorialized in Sir Ninian Comper's fine 'reredos' (carved screen) behind the high altar. The economic basis of the area was now to be found in the factories of Leeds, for the industrial revolution had turned sheep-farming into a business which created a huge export trade in factory-manufactured textiles – but it was felt that the cathedral must be in Ripon. The great west window was given in memory of the first two bishops.

Violent Reactions

An important part of the history of the cathedrals is their ability to arouse hatred and contempt. Of course we are indignant when we read that Protestants wrecked a lovely church in the 16th or 17th century. Crude fanaticism and sheer hooliganism certainly were the evil emotions unleashed in the 1640s as magnificently-coloured windows were broken into fragments, statues of saints beheaded, wall paintings obliterated, tombs rifled, organs silenced, books burned and vestments paraded in mock processions before being cut up. And of course we criticize the Protestant clergy who in later years neglected to keep these churches in repair while they themselves were housed very comfortably. Sections of several cathedrals were let out to local tradesmen and part of Ely Cathedral became a workhouse where the poor were punished for being poor. Our indignation mounts when we are told that gold, jewels and many treasures of medieval art were literally carted off to London, there to be absorbed (and usually lost to sight) in the exchequer of Henry VIII. Twenty-six wagons were needed to take the loot from Becket's shrine in Canterbury. And it is not much of a consolation if we are reminded that vandalism is not confined to one nation, that beauty is never immune, that French revolutionary mobs or the Soviet authorities or the Red Guards in China brutally invaded holy places.

Yet the violence of the reaction against Britain's cathedrals is understandable as something more than an outburst of savagery, and the later refusal to insist on the preservation of these great churches may be interpreted as a verdict on a tradition which had ceased to command respect. For these buildings had flaunted the wealth of the senior clergy, who had not served the people either as pastors or as preachers although they had often been good administrators. Bishops and the heads of cathedrals could be seen as lackeys of the monarch and jumped-up members of the aristocracy. Their ownership of many estates endeared them neither to rival landlords nor to the peasants who sweated on the ground. Already in 1086 when Domesday Book was compiled the Church owned about a quarter of the nation's wealth and as the Middle Ages continued the proportion increased, in popular estimation to a third. A particular grievance about the cathedrals was that they were among the great churches which owned the right to the 'great tithes' of a parish where a 'vicar' or substitute did the priest's work; by 1530 about two fifths of English parishes suffered under this system. (Tithes were a tenth of the annual agricultural produce. The 'great' tithes, to which the 'rector' was entitled, were mainly of corn, hay, wood and fruit. The vicar took what was left.) It is not difficult to understand why complaints erupted into violence, as when the Peasants' Revolt of 1381 ended in the beheading of an Archbishop of Canterbury. In the 1530s the monasteries, including those attached to cathedrals, had few defenders when Henry VIII secured Acts of Parliament dissolving them. In subsequent years many of the bishops' estates were taken from them and fresh violence erupted when the Puritans overthrew and beheaded Charles I in the 1640s. Archbishop Laud's palace in Canterbury was burned down and he was executed; Lichfield Cathedral was bombarded and its bishop's palace was demolished. A riot in favour of the Parliamentary Reform Bill of 1831 set fire to the palace of a Bishop of Bristol, added the cathedral's records to the bonfire and came near to destroying the cathedral. The bishop in Wells might have suffered similarly if he had not drawn up the drawbridge of his moated palace.

In 1547 those who governed England ordered the destruction of all 'monuments of feigned miracles, pilgrimages, idolatry and superstition'. They were placing the power of the State behind a protest which had been first heard in the Lollard movement almost 200 years previously – a protest against the senior clergy's exploitation of the ignorance of the people. Wherever they could manage it, the clergy had put on show a tomb said to be a place of healing miracles. It might be the shrine of one who had been a poor and humble Christian such as St Teilo; or it might contain the body of a boy alleged to have been murdered by Jews (disgracefully, there were such shrines in the cathedrals of Lincoln and Norwich); or its contents might be dubious (three churches claimed to have St Teilo's body and three St Alban's). Even if there was no shrine of a saint to exhibit in return for coins or jewels – in a trade somewhat resembling a modern cinema's – death could be profitable for the clergy. Many of the estates which were given to them were given in exchange for the promise of their prayers after the death of the benefactor. Many smaller gifts were virtually payment for 'indulgences' – the promise of the remission of so many days of punishment in 'penance' on earth or in 'purgatory' on the way to heaven after death. Reputable theologians never endorsed the crude belief that the clergy, if paid to do so, had the power to make God reduce the posthumous punishment for sin. But that certainly was the belief of many simple-minded folk, rich and poor, in the Middle Ages. Guilt and fear were among the foundations of churches great and small.

St Giles

If we go to Scotland we find dramatic evidence of the people's hatred of the racketeering clergy when the storm of the Reformation broke. Glasgow and Kirkwall were the only medieval cathedrals to be preserved (but Glasgow lost its two west towers in the 19th century). In Elgin the whole cathedral, which seems to have had the most sophisticated architecture in medieval Scotland, was allowed to fall into ruin – as was the cathedral of Whithorn, founded by St Ninian in the 5th century (although part of his little stone church has been uncovered by excavation). Elsewhere small cathedrals were made smaller when used as parish churches, as in Brechin, Dunblane and Lismore. In Dornoch in Caithness the 13th-century cathedral was burned out during clan fighting in 1570; in Fortrose most of the stones were used to build Oliver Cromwell's fortifications of Inverness; of St Machar's granite cathedral in Aberdeen, only the nave was left. The cathedral in Dunkeld, which became Scotland's chief church when the Danes sacked St Columba's monastery on Iona, was entirely desecrated in the 16th century although the roof of the choir was replaced in 1600 before it was again devastated, this time by fire, during a battle against the Jacobites in 1689. And in St Andrews the ruins of the once mighty cathedral, and of the archibishop's castle-palace by the sea, provide an even more spectacular monument to the downfall of the medieval Church. Cardinal Beaton was murdered there by Protestants in 1546. But in Scotland we also find a church which was made a cathedral briefly long after the Reformation – and which is also eloquent about the nation's history.

What is properly called the 'high kirk' of St Giles in Edinburgh was a cathedral for only a few years, 1633-39 and 1662-90, when foolish attempts were being made to impose Anglicanism on Scotland. It was founded by Celtic monks (the earliest surviving mention of it comes from 854), but St Giles was a French hermit. The dedication of the Norman church to him, formalised in 1243, tried to stamp a Catholic internationalism on the Scots. And for a time Catholicism did flourish here. Chapels were built by aristocrats or by associations ('guilds') of merchants, and so many of the townspeople endowed 'chantries' for prayers after their deaths that in the end there were some 50 altars.

The 'crowned' stone steeple of St Giles survives as a reminder of pride in the medieval church, which was almost completely rebuilt after being burned by the English in 1385 and extended with a new chancel and clerestory in the 1460s. But Protestantism found a receptive audience in Edinburgh. The statue of St Giles was publicly burned in 1555 and five years later the church was finally stripped of all its Catholic ornaments. Worshippers now sat together at long tables spread with linen to receive the Holy Communion. They also sat under the Protestantism of their new minister, the great preacher and reformer John Knox; he was buried here in 1572. No wonder that a member of the congregation, Jenny Geddes,

threw a stool at the Anglican clergyman when he began to use the Prayer Book ordered by Charles I!

For almost a century and a half after 1560 the future of Scotland remained uncertain and this church was at the heart of the long storm. It knew Mary Queen of Scots, who had come down the 'royal mile' from the palace of Holyrood House, as well as John Knox, her unrelenting critic. It contains monuments to Montrose, Charles I's general in Scotland, and to Argyll, who secured his execution and was executed himself. But in 1603 the two crowns of Scotland and England were united, and in 1707 the two Parliaments, leaving St Giles near the old Parliament House as a shrine where Scotland's history could be recalled in peace. In the great restoration of 1872-83 the partitions which had divided it into three or four separate churches since 1578 were taken down and the whole church was thoroughly repaired. In 1911 a flamboyantly rich chapel designed by Sir Robert Lorimer was opened for the Order of the Thistle, Scotland's equivalent of the Order of the Garter.

Since then, affection has been poured into what one of its ministers has called 'the hospitable home of the Scottish spirit'. In the 1980s a major programme of work included the provision of rooms underground. And people have gone on calling it 'St Giles Cathedral'.

St Giles Cathedral, Edinburgh.

2 THE IDEA OF A CATHEDRAL

Many of Britain's cathedrals have become museums in a sense. They conserve history and art. We go round them hoping that the children will imitate our own hushed voices. Or they may be compared with the great houses now open to the public as stately homes. But here the past has not been fossilized and 'the family' has not been banished to a few rooms. Because it is a building used for something like its original purpose, a cathedral is alive — although it may be (in the words displayed amid the ruins of Glastonbury Abbey) 'a Christian sanctuary so ancient that only legend can record its origins'.

The world of the cathedrals is international. In the Middle Ages kings saw many churches during their constant travelling and could summon architects from far away. (Was Henry 'de Reyns', used by Henry III for Westminster Abbey, English or French? No one knows: his name and his style show a link with Rheims in France, yet he did other work in England and his work in Westminster was far from being entirely French.) In much the same way bishops and the abbots or priors who governed monasteries were internationalists. Bishops represent the unity of the Church, especially if they look to Rome for guidance; abbots or priors are leaders of religious 'orders' with houses in many nations. Such men are not restricted to their own neighbourhoods if they decide to employ architects. (For how long had England been the home of Geoffrey de Noiers, employed by the Frenchman St Hugh on the rebuilding of Lincoln Cathedral? No one knows.) So the cathedrals of Britain may be said to be the symbols of international Catholicism, one dramatic example being the construction of the Norman cathedral on the island of Orkney (then without trees) under the direction of a Norwegian master mason. Although nationalism had its origins in the Middle Ages and the history of English or Scottish architecture reveals this, the word 'catholic' means 'universal' and the bishops' churches proclaim an international faith.

Medieval 'Christendom' was a world of faith. As we have seen, its general credulity encouraged some rackets by the clergy. Another motivation in church-building was a competitive spirit between one place and another. Like a crowd cheering the local team at a football match, a locally-written modern guidebook will not be bashful about local beauty. The Middle Ages were no different. Just inside the door of the chapter house of York are painted words boasting that it is the best, 'as the rose is the flower of flowers'. The bishop (Giles of Bridport) who saw its consecration for worship and now has a fine tomb there boasted that Salisbury was conspicuous 'above all other churches in the world', like the sun amid mere stars. But faith also had a sincere piety which could amount to heroism. About 2,000 years before Christ large 'bluestones' were shipped and hauled from South Wales in order to make a place of worship at Stonehenge in Wiltshire. The coming of Christianity did not mean the end of that instinct. On the contrary, in the Middle Ages the laity often gave willingly to appeals which were not disreputable and the bishops and clergy of cathedrals often taxed their own incomes in order to support funds for the fabrics. We know that Salisbury Cathedral cost about 24,000 marks without the spire, at a time when bishops reckoned that five marks a year was a proper salary for a priest. In 1401 the clergy of Seville Cathedral in Spain resolved to 'build so great a church that those who come after us will think us mad even to have attempted it'.

In medieval England seven of the cathedrals were monasteries in the Benedictine order and under Henry VIII three more such monasteries (in Chester, Peterborough and Gloucester) became cathedrals permanently. Carlisle, Bristol and Oxford Cathedrals were built by canons of the Augustinian order who lived more or less like monks although they also worked in the neighbourhood. In modern times St Albans Abbey and the formerly Augustinian church in Southwark were made cathedrals. In all these great churches, therefore, some impact on the spiritual atmosphere was made by men who had made self-denying vows of individual poverty, chastity and obedience, whatever their corporate wealth might be. Century after century they came into these churches, often in the cold and the dark, in order to pray. Even cathedrals and other great churches which were neither Benedictine nor Augustinian echoed to the frequent sound of chanting in the medieval centuries. In a cathedral such as

Lincoln or Wells it seems to have been normal for more than a dozen canons to be in residence at any one time in addition to the assistant clergy.

In the Middle Ages the chief work of the monks or canons in the cathedrals was the *opus Dei*: the 'work of God' or worship. They recalled Psalm 119 (verse 164): 'Seven times a day do I praise thee'. In particular they chanted a Latin version of the Hebrew psalms over and over again. In our own time their chants, called 'Gregorian' after the pope who sent the first Archbishop of Canterbury to England in 597, are still sometimes used. From the 12th century onwards polyphonic singing and its accompaniment on organs developed. Towards the end of the Middle Ages the growing elaboration of musical 'settings' of the Mass and of appropriate 'anthems' was seen to demand trained choirs of men and boys; the organist was appointed as music master in Salisbury in 1463, and in Lincoln in 1477. After the Reformation this tradition was preserved and developed in England's cathedrals as in few other places in the Christian world. The Book of Common Prayer made provision for anthems 'in Quires and Places where they sing'. The choir schools became training places for musicians whose work might be religious or secular and many of the distinguished composers and instrumentalists of the day were glad to be employed as cathedral organists. And in the 20th century this tradition of choir and organ, with the regular services supplemented by occasional concerts and choir tours, is as vigorous as it has ever been. Twice-weekly broadcasts of Choral Evensong attract and retain audiences which are some of the most appreciative known to the BBC. The cathedrals regularly gather the parish church choirs which are affiliated to the Royal School of Church Music.

Building in Stone

Worship was thought by the people of the Middle Ages to deserve a church built of stone and it has been reckoned that the builders of Salisbury Cathedral used about 120,000 tons of it. For many centuries timber had been the normal building material in Britain and the very old church *(vetusta ecclesia)* at Glastonbury, so old that legend ascribed its construction to Joseph of Arimathea and his fellow-missionaries but destroyed by fire in 1184, was made of wood and wattle. However, already in Anglo-Saxon days kings, nobles and monasteries built stone churches and later wood was thought quite unworthy for use in church-building. And so, without knowing it, the people of the Middle Ages brought into Christian worship the products of the unimaginable ages of evolutionary time.

Cathedrals and other churches were fortunate which stood on or near the great belt of limestone, 140 to 200 million years old, which runs across England from the Dorset coast to the Wash and from Bristol across the Cotswolds to Oxford. Another belt of tough stone runs from Newcastle to Lincoln but this has less lime in it. All limestone was formed by the bodies of tiny sea creatures who once lived in tropical seas or pools. Sediments of their calcium carbonate shells floated to the bottom and acted on sandstone formed by the debris of really ancient rocks. The most prized limestone was Purbeck 'marble' from the Dorset coast. In its natural state (to be seen in Exeter Cathedral) it had various soft colours but it could be polished into a uniform grey or black. Shipped by sea, it was brought up the rivers to the sites where it was wanted to bring colour and drama to duller stone.

If limestone was not available locally it might be imported, and the creamy buff stone of Caen, which hardened on exposure to the air, was valued by Norman church-builders in Kent and East Anglia. It was, of course, far cheaper to use local sandstone, which was often red like the soil of Africa because it, too, was the product of tropical conditions, when a fierce sun beat down on Britain long ages ago. But most sandstone decays more quickly than limestone, as those responsible for the red sandstone cathedrals of Carlisle and Chester, Lichfield and Worcester, have long known to their great cost. Rarer stone suitable for carving included clunch (the soft rock found in chalk) and alabaster (the soft white product of a geological freak quarried in Derbyshire and Staffordshire and fashionable for monuments after 1350). Medieval (not Anglo-Saxon) Englishmen knew how to make bricks, but unlike the Germans and the Italians the English thought that in churches bricks looked unworthy. The Normans' use of Roman bricks in St Albans Abbey was concealed by lime-washed plaster. Much more often the cut stones on the surface concealed rubble which was cemented by mortar which was usually made by heating stones, breaking them into powder and mixing them with sand and water.

A cathedral represents the unity of the universe in stone. The world is perceived not as *chaos* but as *cosmos*. The Greeks who first used these words expressed the geometry in all things when they designed their temples. The medieval Christians, relying on the Bible and the Church as well as on what survived from the ancient world, built churches where everything was in place. Like society as a whole, the church was organized in a hierarchy, from the Pope at the top to the peasant woman or child. Medieval theologians claimed to be able to fit everything in, making a pattern of

18

truths in a hierarchy. So did church-builders. In creating a church a human being can celebrate and even (in a minor way) actually reproduce the achievements of the Architect of the Universe – and it says much about the Christians' God that he is believed to be appropriately worshipped in making beauty. Not only is the church a hall for sacred music which is disciplined so that God, not the singer, is praised; stones, as well as songs, praise this God. The men of the Middle Ages delighted to carve angels playing musical instruments, and architecture itself has been called 'frozen music'. It is no accident that the proportions of a cathedral's architecture can often be analysed mathematically and found to be identical with patterns in the sound of music.

A Towered Cross

In Britain after the arrival of the Normans, a great church was if possible towered like a ladder to heaven, and made 'cruciform' like Christ's cross. Of course a tower had a practical purpose: it was a landmark, which told people where the church was, it advertised the church's importance, and often it housed bells. But we know that monks and other clergy wanted to hold their services beneath a tower which seemed to lift their prayers to heaven. Supporting such a tower depended mainly on the arches beneath it, but was easier if there were strong walls in the 'transepts' or extensions, taking part of the weight. However, the Normans' love of towers was curbed by a series of collapses. Almost all Britain's great towers and stone spires date from the 14th century onwards when building techniques had improved, but even so they have challenged the stability of their churches by their crushing weights. Although some scholars are sceptical about this, the cruciform shape of the church was probably desired for its own sake as a symbol of piety, so that in a building which was full of symbolism (as even the most sceptical scholars agree) the resemblance with Christ's cross was not a coincidence.

The cruciform shape developed from the Roman *basilica*, a long rectangular hall with a timber roof and often with an 'apse' or semicircular end. There the emperor or his local representative dispensed government or justice. In 312 the *basilica* of the imperial palace of the Lateran was converted to use as the cathedral of Rome and so provided a model which, very much adapted and scaled down in its long transition, determined the shape both of the Church of the Nativity in Bethlehem and of the four little Kent churches (in Rochester, Canterbury and Lyminge) which date from 604 to 640. The *basilica* might have had a projecting room, a *porticus*, although there was a great difference between that mere extension and the mighty transepts of a cruciform cathedral. If architecture more ambitious than this timber-roofed basilican style was wanted, a dome could be the chief feature, representing the sky or 'the heavens', in a circular or more or less square building. The Pantheon in Rome was the summit of pagan dome-making and before the beginning of the Italian Renaissance the Christian summit was the dome which dominated *Hagia Sophia* (Holy Wisdom), the 6th-century cathedral of Constantinople or Byzantium (now Istanbul), the capital of the Byzantine (eastern) empire of the Romans. But still Christians wanted cruciform cathedrals. St Mark's sumptuous cathedral in Venice, therefore, had five domes. Solving the problems more simply, the architects of medieval Britain avoided domes. And in the reign of Charles II when Sir Christopher Wren insisted that St Paul's must have a dome, the Anglican clergy replied that the cathedral beneath it must be cruciform, with towers at the west end.

In medieval Britain the altars of a great church faced east. Tradition may well have been an echo of pagan sun-worship; the ruined cathedral of Whithorn in Scotland, founded in the 6th century, is, like the ancient pagan and Christian tombs around it, aligned south-west/north-east, in homage to the midsummer and midwinter solstices. But the practice was justified by the Christian faith that Jerusalem was the world's centre (as Muslims turn towards Mecca in prayer). Often the tradition was refined by making sure that the priest behind the altar would directly face the rising sun on the feast day of the church's patron saint. This love of 'orientation' helps to explain two English traditions diverging from French customs. Transepts were long, with smaller extra transepts towards the east in a few great churches. The east end was usually squared, not semicircular as in the continental 'apse' (which, however, was copied splendidly in Peterborough, Westminster and elsewhere). Both traditions made more east-facing altars possible. Even when the continental custom was accepted and chapels radiated out of the apse somewhat like balloons (this was called a *chevet*), the medieval English liked to have the chapels' altars facing east exactly. We can see that custom in Canterbury or Norwich.

Storied Windows

The light entering a great church was perceived as coming from God. Of course to a religious believer all light has this divine origin, and Sir Christopher Wren, for example, believed that nothing could be more beautiful than the divine gift of plain light. But the men of the

A window made about 1340 for Christ Church Cathedral, Oxford, honours Thomas Becket among other saints.

Middle Ages were fascinated by windows. They were delighted when they found that the small, round-headed window of the Norman building, which seldom contained glass, could be replaced by something far more elegant and comfortable – the 'lancet' window of the Early English style, glazed with stained and painted glass. They were even more pleased when they found that several of these windows could be made very close to each other and that the solid masonry between and around them could have decorative holes cut into it ('plate tracery') and could eventually be replaced by thin bars of stone ('mullions') forming a pattern ('tracery') within one window. By this means what had been separate windows became mere 'lights'. Eventually this technique was applied to towers, so that the windows in them became like arrows shot up to heaven. But of course the chief use of the new windows was to tell stories in glowing colour. John Milton coined the perfect phrase: 'storied windows'.

In the Middle Ages glass was made from potash left by the burning of some woods, mixed with sand. The art of 'staining' it was already known when the monk Theophilus, who was probably a German, wrote his do-it-yourself manual *Diversarium Artium Schedula* about 1120. Molten glass could be coloured blue, green, brown, mauve or ruby by the addition of metallic oxides, but ruby (and sometimes other colours as well) needed to be made less dense by 'flashing', the application of a thin layer of coloured glass to clear glass. The glass was 'grozed' (cut) and painted with a black pigment, as instructed by a 'cartoon' (sketch) prepared by the artist. It was then baked in order to solidify it and was joined with other pieces by lead (and sometimes also by iron). Finally the window was made waterproof by a sealing compound. The medieval English made some glass, but all the best glass was imported to be cut, painted and assembled to their requirements. Stained glass art reached its radiant beauty in its youth, supremely in Canterbury. But later generations learned how to make much larger windows and how to shape the tracery in them in patterns like wheels, roses or hearts. The space between the mullions was now narrower, making story-telling harder, but bits of the glass could be stained with silver chloride which turned yellow when fired, so that portraits could be far more lifelike. Another personal touch was the addition of heraldry, glorifying donors and patrons. The total effect could be much lighter and the custom grew that some of the panes of a window should be left clear. These methods were used in making the windows of the late Middle Ages, supremely in York but also in other centres including London, Norwich, Bristol and Oxford. In the middle of the 16th

century it was discovered that pictures could be painted on clear glass using enamel colours, and this was the beginning of a whole new style of picture-windows.

Often the stories of the Bible and the saints told in these windows could be an instruction or reminder to the illiterate Christian who gazed up in wonder, so that their art provided what was called 'the Bible of the poor'. The parallels between the Old and New Testaments in 'types' and 'antitypes', a favourite theme, must have been expounded frequently. But sometimes the picture would be too high up, or its subject might be too obscure, to tell a story effectively. Its purpose must have been simply the repeating of the story of salvation to the glory of God.

The colour and the stories were not confined to the windows. If we could visit a medieval cathedral as it was, we should be struck – perhaps offended – by the painting or white lime-washing that was everywhere. Often the decoration was in geometric patterns but there were many frescos on the walls, only a few of which have survived sufficiently to be restored. Even the exteriors of churches were often lime-washed. The medieval attitude was that stone, like light, could be improved – perhaps one could say baptized – by colour and art. This delight in pictures of biblical and Christian history contrasts with the tradition of the Jewish synagogue or the Muslim mosque. There, any decoration must avoid portraying people because of the belief that the invisible God alone is to be glorified.

Walls around Worship

Another great contrast exists between the Christian church and the Greek or Roman temple. The temple was built, it seems, chiefly in order to be admired from outside. Inside the divinity would be represented by an impressive statue, but the main impact was made by the front entrance, the 'portico', with its huge columns, and the main altar for sacrifices was usually there. In contrast, the Christian church is built for the congregation around the altar. The worshippers are inspired either by the Bible or by visual story-telling based on the Bible; and the worshippers are inside. Outside, of course, the medieval cathedral is often impressive – but usually the appearance of the exterior is dictated by the needs of the interior.

In the design of the walls of a church the style changed with the changing atmosphere in society as a whole, as we shall see in the next chapter. But the experts warn us against being sentimental. Practical considerations mattered to masons who were workmen, not philosophers. Pointed arches, for example, had an emotional effect but it seems that what was

William Orchard created this vault in Oxford about 1500, above Norman arches in the Transitional style. Much more light could now pour in.

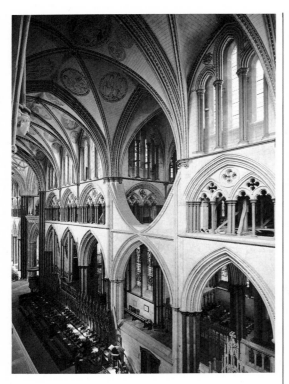

Arches have taken the strain at the base of Salisbury's spire since about 1450.

attractive in the first place was the fact that they were more efficient than rounded arches at carrying loads. Then the gathering of the thrust of the weight of a vault at the bottom of its arches made it possible to insert many more windows into the wall. A wall with big windows would have been unsafe under the continuous weight of the older vaults.

In a great church a wall would have three storeys divided into many 'bays' (vertical units). At floor level extra stability and extra space could be gained by adding a side passage, an 'aisle' (from the old French for 'wing'). This would be behind the main 'arcade' of 'piers' or pillars which supported the wall above them. Above the ceiling of the aisle there could be a lean-to roof which could provide a passageway useful for maintenance (and sometimes, it seems, for extra altars). This passageway and its successors could provide the second storey in the wall. Its usual name since the 19th century has been 'triforium'; the word was first used about Canterbury Cathedral in 1703 and seems to have been derived from the Latin for 'three openings'. However, experts prefer the term 'tribune gallery' when, as in Norman architecture, there is a real passageway with windows and with only one arch matching the arch in the main arcade below. The top storey was the 'clerestory', the clear or light storey whose windows lit the church. It might have a little gallery useful to cleaners. This trio of storeys had a practical purpose, for the shortness of the pillars made the wall more stable, but it provided almost limitless oppor-

tunity for variations in height or lightness or design or ornamentation. In the end the triforium could be reduced to a token or abolished altogether and the aisle could be made the same height as the rest of the nave, in a 'hall church' (as in Bristol Cathedral).

Vault and Buttresses

Despite the English love of length rather than height in a great church, obviously the vault mattered. The wooden ceilings which were all that the Normans could usually manage did not bring their massive walls to much of a climax – and they often caught fire as sparks flew from the houses of wood and thatch surrounding them. But the development of the 'ribbed' vault in stone gave new opportunities to the master masons to reduce the risk of fire and to create new beauty. The innovation was achieved in **Durham Cathedral** early in the 12th century on a scale larger than Christian Europe had seen before. Previously there had been simple, very heavy, semicircular vaults in stone called 'barrel' vaults. There had been 'groin' vaults, where barrel vaults intersected. There had been small experiments in making 'ribs' (arches springing from the four corners) for groin vaults in French churches, the nearest to England being in Bayeux. Rather different experiments had been made by Arab architects in Spain and elsewhere, probably inspired by vaults found in Persia when Islam conquered it. Perhaps the master mason in Durham, whose name is unknown, was a Norman who had learned from one or other of these experiments on the spot. Or perhaps he worked out the new technique for himself. At any rate in Durham the aisles, the choir and the nave were all vaulted in this style and masons all over Europe gradually realised that they had entered a new world. Paul Frankl's magisterial study of *Gothic Architecture* (1962) begins: 'The Gothic style evolved from within Romanesque church architecture when diagonal ribs were added to the groin vault'.

There has been much scholarly argument about whether the ribs in the vaults were mainly useful or mainly decorative. One party points out that when a medieval church is ruined by time or war ribs can stay up when the panels of stone between them have collapsed – to which the reply is that it is not unknown for panels to stay up without ribs. The truth seems to be that this ribbed vaulting is indeed useful. The ribs make the addition of the stone panelling resting on them much easier; they enable spaces of irregular shape to be vaulted; they take the thrust of the ceiling's weight before carrying it downwards. But they are not merely useful. They appeal to religious feelings, for they enable the interior of a church

Flying buttresses across the south aisle of the choir of Gloucester are an early example of the Perpendicular style (about 1350) and help to distribute the great weight above.

to rise to a point where heaven, imagined as being 'up there', is being sought. And they make it possible for masons to raise their imaginations and skills to ever-new achievements in the vaults.

So we get the asymmetrical ribs which were tried out in **Lincoln Cathedral** in the early 1200s and which, although they have little or no practical purpose, are still in place as a talking point about 800 years later. We get a multitude of functionally useless but often enchanting 'tiercerons' and 'liernes'. (The former spring decoratively from the corners of the bay and the latter adorn the crown of the

bay, unconnected with the corners.) In the nave of Lincoln in the 1270s the masons built the first 'star' vaults in Europe. In the cloister of **Gloucester** in the 1350s they ended up with the first 'fan' vaults, where the tracery is all superficial, without any functional purpose but with the power to lift up eyes and hearts. And even this was not the end, as we learn in the little cathedral of **Oxford,** where 'pendants' hung down from the elaborate lierne vaulting – or in Henry VII's chapel in Westminster Abbey, where fan vaulting is above the pendants. The history of vaulting in the great churches of medieval Britain is full of the joy of inventiveness. It cannot be matched in continental Europe.

Medieval builders had to develop an acute understanding of the stresses caused by the raising of great masses of stone high above the earth. Sometimes they underestimated the requirement for strong foundations. Sometimes they overestimated the weight that could be carried by walls or buttresses, so that towers and spires collapsed; William Golding's novel *The Spire* (1964) explores the theme of the clergy's impatient overambition. But far more remarkable than any of the failures is the frequency of success in raising, and keeping up, a building where everything depended on the thrusts of weights being balanced and absorbed.

For example, all the sophisticated beauty of the stone vaults was made possible because the thrust of their weight was largely absorbed by buttresses. In Norman architecture buttresses were hidden within the large gallery, but when Canterbury Cathedral was being rebuilt and extended towards the end of the 12th century another novelty was imported from France – the 'flying' buttress. Now an arch-like structure absorbed the immense weight of the vault and the roof, boldly took it outside the church and carried it safely to the ground. These buttresses could themselves be made beautiful – often with a pinnacle at the top which also had a practical function in that it exerted a vertical thrust. And when roofs were made of lead they were kept in place both by reducing the pitch and by adding a parapet.

Beauty in Wood

Most beauty carved in wood has perished through vandalism or fire. A reminder of what we have lost is the life-sized Mostyn Christ now in Bangor Cathedral, carved about 1500. Once there were wooden statues somewhat like this – although, no doubt, not of the same majesty – in all Britain's churches. Wood that has survived includes sumptuous stalls for the clergy, made from about 1230 onwards. In Salisbury Cathedral these stalls have no canopies at all; in Winchester fairly restrained canopies cover two seats at a time; and then the cascading fireworks in wood begin. They reach a climax of skill and beauty in the achievement of one group of carpenters in Lincoln and Chester between 1370 and 1390.

Often vandals damaged these stalls, but roofs were out of their reach. Here the enemy, often victorious in the Middle Ages, was fire, especially when the roof was covered with wooden shingles before the use of lead (mined in Derbyshire and the Mendips) became common during the 13th century. It is remarkable how many medieval roofs have survived such hazards in parish churches. In the cathedrals there is an especially fine roof in the Durham monks' dormitory, and 'angel' roofs, with merrily painted angels looking down, are spectacular in the transepts of Ely next to that supreme marvel of carpentry, the octagonal roof-lantern.

The cathedral of Bury St Edmunds has a particularly good Victorian version of the 'hammer-beam' roof (where the problems of a large span are reduced by the support of beams which are projected from the walls without meeting). Of such roofs, the supreme medieval example not in a church has survived from the 1390s – Hugh Herland's work for Richard II in Westminster Hall. It was almost contemporary with Ely Cathedral's octagonal lantern. Nor should we forget that above any visible roof or stone vault a lofty roof space is necessary. Here the work of unfailing craftsmanship on the 'rafters' (the beams that make the roof's slope) and other timbers is seen by very few. However, the carpentry is often as extensive as any to be seen in a much-admired 'tithe' barn. So to speak, a gigantic tithe barn is suspended in the sky above the medieval cathedral.

Some of the most skilled carpentry was always dismantled completely and the challenge of reconstructing it in the informed imagination excites modern experts. For, everywhere above a man's height, scaffolding was vital to the work and safety of the masons. Constructing it was all the more difficult because metal nails, then expensive and rare, were not used. The alternative to wooden pegs was lashing by ropes. The difficulty was reduced by projecting scaffolding from poles stuck in the walls, rather than building it up from the ground. This was one of the uses of the triforium or clerestory. There were also many hidden passageways approached by spiral staircases, which eased the problems of maintenance in a great church. Special skills were necessary in the wooden 'centering' which kept the stones of the arches, the ribs and the stone infilling of the vaults, in place until the mortar had set firm after many months. What was almost a whole temporary church in wood, technically called 'falsework', had to precede whatever might be built in stone.

3 THE CLERGY

Nowadays cathedrals are often called people's churches. The clergy enthusiastically call them that. But it is significant that medieval churches were usually built from east to west because the eastern part was the clergy's and that was thought to be more urgent. Later, this part was often pulled down because the clergy wanted something more modern and spacious. The nave could be left and its west front could be built with architecture usually much inferior to the glories around the clergy. In his study of church life in England, *The Later Middle Ages* (1979), J. C. Dickinson realistically observed that 'the role of the medieval cathedral in local church life was far less prominent than is now habitual, partly because of the over-large size of most dioceses and the poor communications, but also because of the great strength of local parish life'.

The Bishop

The chief priest was the bishop, whose main residence or 'palace' was often the cathedral's nearest neighbour. It could be a spectacular and fortified building – most memorably Durham Castle and the moated palace of Wells. The comparatively poor bishops of St David's built a stately home for themselves in a Welsh village almost within sound of the Atlantic. Inside the cathedral the bishop's throne was prominent, either through its central position (preserved in Norwich and recently revived in Canterbury) or through its size and superb carving (as in Durham or Exeter). From the cathedral's point of view the bishop often earned his throne and tomb, for again and again in the architectural history we find the bishop as initiator. No doubt a bishop who is said to have 'built' or 'rebuilt' a cathedral did not pay for it all, any more than he worked on it with his own hands. And no doubt he was not unmindful of the credit he would acquire personally. But the reconstruction of Exeter Cathedral in a consistent style was the result of initiative and persistence by five successive bishops between the 1270s and the 1370s. Thanks to them this church, which was not one of the richer cathedrals in the Middle Ages, was one of the most glorious. And that example is not unique.

Around the living bishop were monuments to his predecessors and every effort was made to secure the recognition ('canonization') of at least one of them by the Pope as a saint, whose shrine could be placed behind the high altar with all possible splendour. Such a saint could not attract quite the devotion which would be given to any relic associated with the Bible (for example, the Holy Shroud in Turin or the Crown of Thorns in Paris or the *sancta camisia*, a piece of the garment which was believed to have been worn by the Virgin when giving birth to Christ and which was the chief treasure of Chartres). But a sainted bishop's body was still something fascinating in the Middle Ages – and something far more popular than the jurisdiction exercised by his living successor.

In **St David's**, village and cathedral alike are named after a 6th-century bishop. His memory was honoured continuously after his death but the pilgrimage began to bring real wealth only from the 12th to the 16th century. Then pride in *Dewi Sant* was officially permitted, even encouraged, and it served as a way of expressing the spirit of Welsh Christianity under English rule. Paradoxically, English craftsmen seem to have been imported in order to create some of the splendour of St David's Cathedral – the Norman nave, the Decorated windows which ended the darkness, the stalls for bishops and canons in warmly glowing oak, the richly-panelled wooden ceilings, the chapels, the tower raised to its present height not long before the Reformation. It was the Welsh equivalent of the Spanish Santiago de Compostela near the Atlantic 400 miles to the south, the great centre of pilgrimages to the shrine of St James the apostle, reputed to have been buried there and to have appeared again as a warrior to save Spain from the Moors.

In England sainted bishops seem to have owed much of their popularity to their Englishness in times when the ruling class, which was essentially a military caste, spoke French and essentially was French in culture. So the English people flocked to St Cuthbert of Durham, St Chad of Lichfield, St Swithun of Winchester and the two Saxon saints of Worcester. They honoured bishops involved in defiance of the monarchy, supremely St Thomas of Canterbury but also St Thomas of Hereford,

27

or bishops who had devoted themselves to pastoral work among them such as St Hugh of Lincoln (an honorary Englishman) or St Richard of Chichester. And memories have not completely died. But the attempts of some cathedrals to put their own bishops into the same prestigious and profitable class have not met with permanent success. Who now associates London with St Erkenwald?

No woman could be ordained but the people of the Middle Ages honoured some women saints, royal as well as holy, such as St Etheldreda the virgin queen, all ice and fire, who founded Ely Cathedral, or St Werburg, a Mercian princess whose relics were brought to Chester Cathedral early in the 10th century. When a great church could not exhibit a plausible saint's shrine something was missing. It was a nagging problem for York and Wells amid their splendours, and it irritated the canons of Salisbury that Osmund, their bishop who died in 1099, was not recognized in Rome as a saint until 1453, although they began their petitions in 1228.

Around the bishop other clergy gathered as his *familia* or household. In the simple early days the cathedral's clergy were the bishop's close associates in his missionary and pastoral work and in the worship which inspired and refreshed it, which explains the tradition that a new bishop should be elected by the cathedral's clergy. The tradition caused innumerable disputes in the Middle Ages, when both the King and the Pope claimed rights more weighty than the cathedral's; but it has survived in the Church of England's curious practice of inviting the cathedral's clergy to 'elect' a bishop whose name has already been decided. And the idea that the cathedral was still essentially the bishop's church even survived developments which distanced the bishop from it.

He became busy elsewhere. His 'diocese' (a word significantly derived from a division of the Roman empire) was large in England and Wales – much larger than in Scotland or France, Italy or Greece – because its size was usually suggested by the earlier division of the country into tribal kingdoms. In England before the 1540s the only dioceses which a modern bishop would regard as manageable were Canterbury, Rochester and Ely. When the Middle Ages ended there were still only 17 dioceses and about three times as many clergy to cover about 9,500 parishes. At an early stage of the Reformation Henry VIII wrote out a list of 21 large churches which would make extra cathedrals, but it was only a passing thought: the new dioceses which he actually founded were a quarter of that number. The medieval bishop delegated most of the routine administration to his 'vicar general', a priest who in

his absence supervised the diocese and who might be a canon of the cathedral, to his 'official' (later 'chancellor') who dealt with legal matters, and to the 'archdeacons', whose chief task was to inspect the parish churches (in theory every year); and these in turn delegated much of the work to their own officials. For services which needed a bishop, such as ordinations and confirmations, assistant bishops were employed (often Irish), with titles derived from dioceses outside England; these were the predecessors of the modern 'assistant', 'suffragan' or 'area' bishops. In effect an ecclesiastical civil service developed to cope with the large dioceses. But that did not leave the bishop idle.

In the Middle Ages – as in earlier Anglo-Saxon days – the bishop was often expected to immerse himself in what today would be regarded as the business of politicians and civil servants, for he could be a minister of the King. In royal eyes this was a convenient arrangement, for the bishop had to provide his share of knights or taxes for the army yet was paid out of ecclesiastical revenues and was prohibited by ecclesiastical rules from having legitimate children who might distract him from his obligation to give priority to the interests of the Crown. Even if he was not employed by the King, he had to keep his eye on non-ecclesiastical matters. In a chapel of **Chester Cathedral** the simple wooden fittings of a 'consistory' court survive. Here the bishop's principal legal officer, the chancellor, would hear cases involving not only religious and moral questions – an allegation of heresy or absence from church, for example, or a charge that someone had defamed a neighbour or carried friendship to the point of fornication – but also problems to do with marriages and wills. This courtroom was made in the 1630s and is a reminder that still in that century bishops could be significant and powerful in the State as well as in the Church.

Whether or not ecclesiastical or secular

business pressed on the bishop, one duty was clear throughout the Middle Ages and later. He and his large staff (including knights, who were bodyguards) had to keep moving from house to house in the diocese or further afield, either in order to attend meetings, councils, festivities at court or sessions of Parliament, or in order to conduct 'visitations' or inspections throughout the diocese, or in order to hold ordinations and confirmations, or simply in order to consume the produce of the bishop's estates which could not easily be brought to the cathedral city. In the Middle Ages to be a bishop was to be a man constantly on horseback.

Monks and Canons

The cathedral clergy's sense of themselves as a distinct community increased as the bishops withdrew. A great church could be called in Latin a *monasterium*, Anglicized as 'Minster', whether or not it was staffed by monks (as Westminster was but as York Minster was not). In the great churches which actually were monasteries worship was offered in at least seven services a day interspersed with periods of manual, literary or administrative work. Combining a cathedral with a monastery was almost unknown in continental Europe but the Normans found that the arrangement had been begun in Anglo-Saxon Winchester, and it appealed to them and to their successors. The monastery's wealth could be diverted to help the bishop's finances. Thus the creation of the diocese of Ely in 1109 was made possible by appointing a bishop as abbot and allowing him to keep most of the wealth. At one stage East Anglia's bishop tried to take over the rich monastery of Bury St Edmunds but was repelled, as was Somerset's bishop when he tried to take over Glastonbury. Additionally, the monks' ordered round of worship and work provided a respectable setting for the bishop's most public appearances. But inevitably there were often tensions between monks and bishops. The medieval history of the great monastic cathedrals of Canterbury and Durham, to cite only two examples, is full of such disputes. In two dioceses the bishops preferred cathedrals with canons to churches with monks, which had at least an equal claim to dignity but whose monks insisted on their own ways; they preferred Wells to Bath and Lichfield to Coventry. Even if there was harmony – a collaboration which could result in the enrichment of the church architecturally – the monks remained conscious that they had interests and duties which were not the bishop's. The cathedral monastery was a complicated business concern as well as a house of prayer. Its prior, who was the bishop's deputy at the head of the monks, became a

significant figure in his own right, responsible for the oversight of many estates and mixing hospitably with fellow-landowners. A prior such as Henry of Eastry, who between 1285 and 1331 ran Canterbury Cathedral, its monastery and its estates, did not stand in awe of any archbishop.

It has often been felt that responsibility for a rich cathedral was bad for the monks. That is no doubt true if one understands a monk's life in terms of the document which was, in theory, authoritative, the 'rule' of St Benedict, compiled about 530. In this rule monks were expected to be poor men working with their hands. Most would be laymen and most would be young. But such evidence as there is suggests that monasteries which were not cathedrals in the Middle Ages experienced much of the same decline in spiritual creativity as the rich cathedrals when they were weakened by the staleness which came with time or were burdened with the cares which came with wealth. At least the Benedictine rule, read to the monks day by day over 1000 years, was always a reminder of the old ideal.

In the non-monastic or 'secular' cathedrals, the collective term for a group of 'canons' was (and is) 'chapter', although there was no rule of life to be read chapter by chapter. The statutes of these cathedrals were largely a development of those drawn up by a Bishop of Salisbury, Osmund, in 1091. They provided for a dean or chairman, a precentor in charge of the worship, a chancellor who supervised the correspondence, library and records and any grammar school in the diocese, and a treasurer responsible for finances and valuables.

In addition to these dignitaries, who often appointed deputies to do most of the work, there were many other canons or prebendaries. In Lincoln, where a different canon was supposed to conduct the services during each week of the year and 110 stalls were needed in order to seat them and their deputies, statutes revised in 1440 were badly needed in the very difficult attempt to regulate the 'chapter'. The canons of Salisbury or Wells were approximately as numerous. When in residence canons were expected to be hospitable, which could be an expensive business. They lived in their own houses, or shared, and were financed out of estates or tithes, the 'prebends' attached to their positions in the church. The names of the places which supplied the canons' stipends can still be found written up over the stalls in the choirs of some cathedrals.

It was a system open to many abuses. The value of a prebend varied according to the cathedral and the stall within it. In general only the four dignitaries were highly paid. They still considered themselves entitled to supplement their incomes by other posts in Church and

State, as the other, lesser, canons also did if they had the chance, residing in the cathedral seldom or never. So the cathedral came to be regarded as a collection of part-time incomes. Appointments were made, by Pope, King or bishop, of men who were not priests or not English, purely for the sake of the income, but the positive value of this arrangement was that the cathedral could subsidise administrators, pastors or scholars who made themselves useful elsewhere.

The custom that the canons were entitled to appoint 'vicars' or substitutes to sing the services in their absence grew, and gradually these deputies received their own definite pay, accommodation and common life. They were housed in the Vicars' Close in Lichfield, in a whole cloister surviving in Hereford and in a whole street in Wells. Towards the end of the Middle Ages the cathedrals also contained a considerable number of 'chantry' priests whose duty was to pray for the souls of benefactors. In York 24 such priests were housed in St William's College. About a century before that there had been no fewer than 74 chantry priests in St Paul's Cathedral. St Paul's was also exceptional in that not one of the 'vicars choral' was a priest, but there was a fully constituted and properly paid college of priests who were 'minor canons', a dozen in number.

The criticism that the medieval cathedral had too large a staff is evidently justified. But one institution which was at the margin of its life in the Middle Ages has turned out to be of unquestionable benefit to many boys – the school. The scholars among the early bishops were expected to be educators and the Anglo-Saxon cathedrals of Canterbury and York (to mention only two) were places where future priests were taught. Later every cathedral had a school of some sort and some bishops, most notably of Winchester, and deans, most notably of St Paul's, founded schools which were far more elaborate. Lincoln was a cathedral whose chancellor organised education at several levels. These were the foundations on which, in a number of cathedrals, a later 'King's School' would be built on the orders of Henry VIII. He allocated to this cause a small portion of the revenues of the monastery he had dissolved.

In his reign the cathedrals which had been monasteries ceased to be so, although not a few of the priors carried on as deans, some of the monks became canons and the rest received pensions if they accepted the settlement, as almost all of them did. Six great churches which had been Benedictine or Augustinian became the cathedrals of new dioceses although the new use for Westminster Abbey lasted for only ten years, 1540-50. Each cathedral was placed under a Dean and Chapter, the latter consisting of 'residentiary' canons. The corporate life of all the cathedrals now became much the same, with most of the clergy being married and many of them, especially the deans, being appointed by the Crown. Nowadays the dean and two canons are paid by the Church Commissioners. There are also honorary canons (or prebendaries), parish priests whom the bishop wishes to honour.

There are differences in fame and wealth between cathedrals and the 'statutes' or constitutions under which they are administered are not identical. However, the Anglican cathedral is a recognizable development of the last four centuries. It has produced a life of its own, fascinating many novelists. It has remained recognizable, although again different from place to place, when in the 19th and 20th centuries some parish churches have been given an extra role as Anglican cathedrals without ceasing to be parish churches. (The priest presiding over them is called the 'provost' not the 'dean', is appointed by the bishop not the Crown and is also the 'rector' or 'vicar' of the parish.) The degree of independence which the clergy of Anglican cathedrals have enjoyed and sometimes abused can be seen as a survival from the Middle Ages when the bishop was not in effective daily control. By contrast the Roman Catholic cathedrals have resulted from the 'restoration of the hierarchy' in the middle of the 19th century. The bishops, appointed by the Pope, control their own cathedrals in some detail. The senior priest is called merely 'the administrator' and the work of the cathedral is mainly the work of an active parish church.

The fact that in medieval Britain the emphasis was on the cathedral clergy as a large and semi-detached community explains some features which distinguish the cathedrals of this country from most of those of continental Europe. French Gothic cathedrals are often much higher than any medieval church in Britain (in Beauvais the distance from floor to vault is almost 48 metres or 158 feet, double what the English liked) and they rise dramatically in the midst of busy streets. But the English tradition, copied in Scotland and Wales so far as resources permitted, was to spend money on length, not height. Winchester Cathedral, for example, is 30 metres (100 feet) longer than Germany's longest, Cologne.

One reason for making long naves was that they could house altars; in St Albans medieval wall paintings show where the altars were. But the length was mainly due to the requirement for space in which the clergy could walk in solemn processions on Sundays and other festivals. In the Middle Ages the naves of cathedrals and monasteries never had chairs in them, although as a concession there might be

a stone bench by the wall (hence the saying 'the weakest go to the wall'). And the nave was definitely separated from the choir where the monks or canons held their main services. To mark the division the builders in the 14th and 15th centuries often built a stone screen or *pulpitum* (a Latin word originally meaning a stage used by actors), which might include other altars and provide a platform for singers. There would often also be a wooden screen, a 'rood', supporting a sculpture of the Crucifixion of Christ with his mother and St John beside him. It became the custom to bring the saint's shrine up from the crypt to a position behind the high altar, and as devotion to the Blessed Virgin Mary intensified the bishop and clergy built an elaborate Lady chapel right at the east end. So the long sprawl of the cathedral increased.

Another characteristic of the old English cathedral is its detachment from the life of the town, whether or not it was a monastery. It formed a village on its own. If funds and the King permitted, it could be surrounded by an encircling wall, making a 'Close' or 'Precincts' or 'College'. There was also usually a courtyard or 'cloister' (from the Latin *claustrum*, or 'enclosed place'), with covered walks enclosing a central space or 'garth'. In Salisbury Close there were no monks but there was the largest cloister in the country, for a cloister seemed appropriate, however expensive.

The cloister usually led to the 'chapter house', uniquely prominent in England and so called because a chapter of the rule of St Benedict was read to monks every day. Here the monks were supposed to confess their sins to each other and to receive admonition before transacting the business of the day. The canons of a secular cathedral met in roughly the same way, although less often and without the confession of sins. Even in great monasteries chapter houses were often quite small rooms, but it was often thought that the dignity of a cathedral demanded a separate building. Worcester Cathedral had a circular house, with a central pillar to support the vault, built about 1150, and at Lincoln the chapter house had ten sides. But Westminster Abbey (about 1250) made eight sides what the cathedral clergy wanted unless they were content with a very large rectangular room with a spectacular vault, as they were in Canterbury.

4 THE LAITY

King John wished to be buried near the saints of Worcester.

So the bishop and the monks or canons dominated the medieval cathedral. But of course the laity were also essential to its life from the day when the first stone was laid. The Normans often made the principal town in a district the site of a new cathedral, abandoning the village or smaller town which had been the base of the Anglo-Saxon bishop. Decided at a council held in Windsor in 1072, this policy was in part motivated by the fear that a bishop's cathedral in an unfortified place might be burned down by English rebels. A cathedral seemed to need a castle near it even if there was no surrounding town (as in Old Sarum). But normally after 1072 the cathedral and the town grew together.

A town could be called a 'city' if it contained a cathedral and the cathedral became a centre of civic life. The nave, although built primarily for the purposes of the clergy, was also a large hall where the laity from the city and the surrounding countryside could assemble. It was the custom for pious folk who lived within a convenient distance to go there for Mass carrying offerings on Whitsunday, the birthday of the Christian Church. It was also the custom to use the nave as a meeting place for business and social purposes and as the scene of a big event such as a trial. The evidence for such use is strongest in the case of St Paul's Cathedral but presumably the custom was not confined to London. In the stained glass of Chartres Cathedral 42 different trades announce that the gift is theirs with more than 100 scenes showing their different occupations – the world's most glorious commercial advertisement. Although Britain cannot now produce similar proof of the involvement of the medieval laity, we have no reason to suppose that the situation was totally different in this country. In York Minster a window depicts the art of bell-making and includes a portrait of Richard Tunnoc, goldsmith, bell-founder and benefactor, buried nearby in 1330. And we know that in many cathedrals there was a stream of pilgrims visiting the shrine of the local saint, walking along an 'ambulatory' so as not to disturb the monks or clergy in the choir and presbytery.

The King and the People

The most important layman was, of course, the King. Medieval kings and princes often stayed

in monasteries, including those attached to cathedrals, partly because these were the best hotels available but also in order to exercise their piety, genuine or assumed. They left behind generous gifts at the saint's shrine and sometimes their own bodies were buried in the cathedral. William Rufus was buried in Winchester and King John in Worcester. Henry IV and the Black Prince were buried near St Thomas in Canterbury. The tomb of Edward II, who had been murdered like St Thomas, itself became a shrine in Gloucester. The tomb of St Edward the Confessor was surrounded by many other royal tombs in Westminster Abbey, from Henry III onwards; while the very name of Bury St Edmunds shows that the body of a young Christian king killed by the Vikings in 870 was the chief treasure of that very rich monastery in Suffolk from the 10th century onwards. And on the fringe of the medieval world the cathedral of Kirkwall was built as the shrine of a candidate for the earldom of Orkney, St Magnus, murdered in 1137.

Cathedrals delighted to exhibit proofs of royal or princely patronage; the sculptures on the west fronts of Wells and Exeter include many kings while others guard the great stone screens in Canterbury and York. This tradition went back a long way in European history. In 306 Constantine the Great, who became the first Christian to exercise supreme political power, was proclaimed emperor by his troops

The Norman nave of Ely with its Victorian painted roof.

in the Roman military headquarters on the site where York Minster was later built. The medieval emperor Charlemagne, crowned in Rome in 800, was the centre of a cult in the cathedral at Aachen, and Cologne Cathedral was even more ambitious in its consecration of the Holy Roman Empire by developing the cult of the Magi, regarded as three kings who were received by the infant Christ. In France the monarchy owed a great deal to the sacredness imparted by the Church and, in return, royal patronage was vital in the history of cathedral architecture. In England the link between Crown and Church was intimate from the beginning when missionary bishops converted Anglo-Saxon kings. From Elizabeth I onwards every monarch has been 'Supreme Governor' of the Church of England as well as 'Defender of the Faith', and the Christian character of the monarchy is dramatized in the tradition that the Sovereign distributes 'Maundy money' every Maundy Thursday in a cathedral or Westminster Abbey.

Laity who were not royal have also left their identifiable marks on the cathedral. Tombs of lords, knights and ladies handsomely preserve for us something of the life of the medieval aristocracy. Countless monuments on the walls of cathedrals and other churches constitute a history of the gentry in later centuries. Ordinary medieval life is reflected more cheerfully in the tradition that the 'gargoyles', the stone water-spouts on the roof, and the 'corbels', or other projecting blocks of stone, could be carved in the shapes of men and animals, often grotesque. It was also the custom that 'misericords', the little tip-up seats on which the clergy could rest during the long services, had carvings beneath them and more than 700 survive in English cathedrals. These carvings seldom had a religious subject or any particular scheme. They were copied from books or carved at the carpenter's whim, it seems. Many were comic – in Bristol a man and wife quarrel over a cooking pot, in Worcester a nude woman rides a goat – and those which do not raise a smile often show the countryman's unsentimental delight in animals, including in Exeter an elephant given to Henry III.

The tops ('capitals') of piers, the central stones or pieces of wood in the vaulted ceilings, and the chapter houses were also places sufficiently far from the sanctuary to make it possible for the carving sometimes to avoid piety. The merry imp who lowers the tone of the Angel Choir in Lincoln is almost as famous as the cathedral itself. In Wells the peasant complaining about toothache, or the man removing a thorn from his foot, or the gossip with a bridle to shut her mouth, arouses an almost equal affection. And Wells has a little series of capitals showing grape-stealing and its

Misericords – the little seats used by the clergy for resting during a long service. The 13th-century elephant is in Exeter and the injured knight is in Lincoln.

chastisement. Medieval England was warm enough to grow grapes.

Medieval daily life is also exhibited on many of the bosses in the cathedrals of Exeter and Norwich and the leaves carved around the chapter house of Southwell are admired as the best possible proof of the stonemason's power to translate what he saw with his eyes into what he did with his hands. In Carlisle capitals carved early in the 14th century depict the pleasures and labours of the months – January feasting, February warming by the fire, March digging, April pruning, May admiring the blossom, June hawking, July mowing, August working in the fields, September reaping, October harvesting grapes, November sowing, and December slaughtering an ox for Christmas. A similar scheme was worked out in wood in Worcester's misericords.

The Craftsmen

It was rare, although not unknown, for monks or canons to be themselves artists or craftsmen. Usually they designated one of their number as 'warden' or *custos fabricae* and through him they employed masons and other craftsmen at the going rates of pay, for the building of a big church was no work for amateurs. The 'windlasses' or treadmills which hauled the stones up by ropes to build or repair the cathedrals at Peterborough and Salisbury, and which have survived, are among the sights which remind us that medieval church-building needed both the skills acquired through long experience and hard physical labour. Much of the evidence suggests that the clergy left the craftsmen largely to themselves once the basic style, theme and extent of the work had been agreed. Glaziers, for example, were paid by the square foot for their creations which seem to us magical and priceless.

The craftsmen were prepared to work 12 hours a day in the summer, beginning at 5 o'clock, although they stopped for the weekend and any 'holy day' of the Church (of which there was, averaged through the year, one a week). They could be laid off from October to May, when the building site would be deserted and the unfinished work covered with straw; then they had to manage with farm work back home. Stonemasons were likely to be afflicted by arthritis because they worked outside in the rain and to die of silicosis because of the stone dust. Carpenters, although sheltered from rain and dust, did not enjoy rates of pay at all in keeping with their skill; the two men, Robert and William, who made the 18 metre (60 feet) high throne of the Bishop of Exeter in 1317 were paid a little less than two thirds of the cost of the wood. But these men had their pride. They were workmen who often knew each other well, moving about the country from one job to another. They shared dangers at work and lodgings in the evening. Perils and fellowship are on record in a bracket preserved in the south transept of Gloucester Cathedral (although the image which supported it has gone). A young man is shown falling to his death from the vault, while the bearded master mason looks on in horror. This may well be a memorial to one of the tragedies which brought home the costs of these immensely ambitious masterpieces of co-ordinated craftsmanship.

Both standards of craftsmanship and rates of pay were protected by excluding amateurs. Although the origins of modern freemasonry in the 17th century are unclear, there must have been some connection with the 'free' or 'banker' masons who cut or carved the stones and were superior to the 'rough' or 'setting' masons who carried them to the site and set them in mortar. In the later Middle Ages masons organized themselves more or less on trade union lines and strikes seriously delayed the completion of York Minster. The mason's best friend was the Black Death, the plague which first struck in the 1340s; the population went down, and masons' wages up, by about a third. But there is no reason to doubt that the masons had other motives for work in addition to wage-earning. They worked carefully for places where their work would seldom be seen – for example, intricately carved 'bosses' were placed in vaults 18-21 metres (60-70 feet) above any spectator. The skills of 'the Craft' were transmitted almost entirely by word of mouth in 'the lodges', often from the father to the son, always from the skilled craftsman to the apprentice who must produce his 'master-piece' in order to qualify. Almost all the names of these men have been lost, although masons' marks have often been left on the stones (in

Peterborough Cathedral there are more than 100 different marks), many of them probably made by apprentices so that their work could be checked.

The Master Masons

The 'master masons' were not architects quite as we understand that profession, for in youth they had been practical masons rather than students. But they were important men. Many of their names are known. One of them with his iron L-square (incorporating a ruler marked with inches) and compass or dividers (for drawing circular lines) still looks down from the nave of Peterborough where he was painted in the 1220s. Sculptured heads of laymen to be seen on the walls of the cathedrals of St Albans, Wells and Exeter may be portraits of master masons (Henry Wy, Adam Lock and Thomas of Whitney) although we cannot be sure. A drawing in a book made in St Albans shows a master mason arguing with a king and we know that in the later Middle Ages master masons as distinguished as Henry Yvele and his great rival William Wynford often dined with bishops. Such men were paid at least three times the average mason's wages, with special contracts that often enabled them to supervise more than one project at the same time. They had to be organizing executives, gathering all the necessary timber and stone (with primitive transport at a high cost) and hiring and disciplining a large labour force. And they had to be planners combining a creative imagination with a never-failing practicality. In York and Wells rooms have survived which show how the shaping of wood and stone was ordered. 'Templates' (pieces of wood or metal) were cut to sizes determined by lines drawn on plaster.

Although much has been learned about building methods from a close study of the building accounts which survive – most notably from Henry III's reconstruction of Westminster Abbey – almost all the plans and all the models used when building Britain's medieval churches have perished. Three architectural drawings in a 14th-century sketch book now in Magdalene College, Cambridge, are not much. Fortunately the rest of Europe provides more evidence. There are some small paintings in 'illuminated' manuscripts where the Tower of Babel and Solomon's Temple were favourite subjects. Careful drawings survive which are designs for the cathedrals of Rheims, Cologne, Strasbourg and Vienna. We have the sketchbook of one master mason, Villard de Honnecourt, who in the 13th century worked in Hungary as well as in France, and we can read the minutes of the committee which in the 1380s and 1390s argued about plans for the building of Milan Cathedral.

5 SINCE THE MIDDLE AGES

The choir and clergy of Ripon Cathedral. Singing has always been an important part of a religious service.

The development of building technology is not the only sign in the old cathedrals that the Middle Ages are moving towards the modern world. We may notice an old clock in Salisbury, Wells, Exeter or Durham, or the medieval map of the world in Hereford, and feel that the modern obsessions with time and travel are starting. In Lincoln and Salisbury are two of the four oldest surviving copies of the Magna Carta. Contemplating them, we glimpse the beginnings of modern freedom, and understand why in 1279 Archbishop Pecham ordered that a copy of Magna Carta should be placed in every cathedral in England.

The Protestant Reformation

For more than 300 years after the barons had extracted Magna Carta from King John such elements of modernity were held within a very firm structure, the society called Christendom. But the medieval union of faith and knowledge, church and realm, patron and artist, did not last. In **King's College Chapel** in Cambridge we see it dying splendidly. The basic design of the great windows is medieval; the Old Testament is spread like a rich canopy above the life of the Virgin and her Son, from biblical or legendary sources. Everything is theologically orthodox. But the pictures, wonderfully coloured, physically energetic as they largely ignore the dividing mullions, are in much the same style as the frescoes being painted on European walls by Michelangelo and lesser artists. Costumes and scenery belong to the Renaissance and the Church's control over all this vitality seems more fragile than the glass. When the glaziers were told to stop work in the 1530s they had not got round to the west window. The next craftsmen employed in the chapel were to carve emblems celebrating the marriage of Henry VIII with Anne Boleyn. England's Renaissance prince had triumphed.

Already within the Middle Ages some laymen were impatient with the kind of knowledge that was stored in cathedral libraries and communicated in cathedral schools. One reason why medieval Oxford and Cambridge attracted the students who began universities was that these towns contained no bishops and no cathedrals. Bishops and cathedral monasteries founded colleges when they

recognized the new phenomenon and theology was 'queen of the sciences' in what the universities taught. However, the protests of an Oxford theologian, John Wyclif, at the end of the 14th century were not isolated as signs of tension between teachers and bishops – a quarrel which could be taken direct to the people, with an open Bible in the people's language (as Wyclif and his followers the Lollards took it). Then, from about 1530, the Protestant Reformation erupted. It still belonged to the ages of faith, as can be seen from the new prominence of the pulpit where the clergy preached to the people, but its rebellion against the higher clergy eventually turned into a rebellion against orthodox Christianity itself. Cathedrals which had been the birthplaces, or at least the showpieces, of many technical and artistic advances now suffered from brutal vandalism, damaging neglect and the name 'Gothic'.

The term 'Gothic' was derived from vague memories of the Visigoths, barbarian invaders who had wrought havoc in central Europe and had swept down into Italy, sacking Rome in 410. 'Goths' was a word used contemptuously by, for example, Giorgio Vasari, about 1550. He was one of a chorus of pundits of the Italian Renaissance who blamed the decadence of medieval architecture – 'not architecture but confusion' declared Anderea Palladio – on German influences. It was alleged that the Goths, or at any rate the Germans, had invented the pointed arch by tying together trees which they were unable to cut down. The simple but

The Eucharist is celebrated among the people in Ripon. Only part of the great arch above was remodelled in the Perpendicular style before the end of the Middle Ages.

grand symmetry of Ancient Rome was preferred, in the style which came to be called Palladian. In the 17th century, which became the 'Age of Reason', Molière condemned the 'odious monstrosities of an ignorant age' and the term 'Gothic' came into use in Britain, where Sir Henry Wotton despised the 'imbecility' of the pointed arch and John Evelyn called medieval architecture 'fantastical and licentious'. Although a few neo-medieval buildings were still being designed and constructed in an unbroken tradition (the 'Gothic survival'), fashionable people now thought that medieval churches represented the very 'chaos' and 'barbarism' which they had been designed to contradict.

New Love and Life

Beginning within the 18th century, there was a reaction in favour of the Gothic style – the 'Gothic revival'. At first it was a hobby of the few, little more than a scholarly interest in antiquity or a romantic taste for a change from classical, cosmopolitan Palladianism. In an essay of 1772 the young Goethe defended the Gothic style precisely because it was German and it was not long before its buildings were being praised because they had grown and branched like trees in a forest. Some damage was done by restorers who were too confident about how the Middle Ages ought to have built, but gradually their admirers gained appreciation of how they actually had built. All the old cathedrals of England and Wales were included among the innumerable churches which were restored. New cathedrals were built in a neo-medieval style. That story belongs to our next chapter, but here we may note that for much of the 19th century the Church of England still regarded cathedrals as churches chiefly used by the clergy and for robed choirs who sang Matins and Evensong every day. Congregations could sometimes be large; a Sunday evening service in a gas-lit nave could draw a crowd. Tourism also increased with the development of the railways. But the normal impression of a Victorian cathedral was that it was nobly silent – beautiful, but still a backwater, costing sixpence to enter. In 1836, protesting against proposed legislation, the Dean and Chapter of Winchester defended cathedrals as 'retreats of learned leisure, where, free from the anxieties attendant upon a narrow income, and from the incessant cares which belong to the cure of souls, they could give themselves more entirely to the higher walks of literature and theology'. Such a defence did not persuade many of the laity. Reformers argued about whether the canons ought to be scholars and teachers or diocesan officials but it was usually assumed that between Matins and Evensong there was a prospect of idleness if the clergy confined their attention to the cathedral. Only slowly in the Victorian Age was it seen that the cathedral could itself be a place for hard work.

Gradually in the modern age the cathedrals have burst into life. They have been used as popular theatres and visited as tourist attractions to an extent which no previous century ever imagined. Service on their staffs is no longer often a temptation to idleness. Some cathedral clergy are scholars but few of them can fairly be called leisured. Of course, each cathedral has its own history of development and the particular balance between local use and tourism varies from place to place, but all these great and busy churches often welcome crowds attending a special service sponsored by a diocesan or national society, or a carol service before Christmas, or some other celebration (for example, by young people), or a concert of sacred music – and the increase of mobile leisure has greatly increased the number of visitors. In the 1830s, as the historian Owen Chadwick has written, 'no one knew what a cathedral was for'. By the 1980s the cathedral had become the Church's shop window. And when they come people do not expect to feel in any way excluded.

Changing attitudes have left their mark on the cathedral's appearance. Shops, restaurants, toilets, car parks and explanatory notices are the signs of a practical understanding of the needs of tourists, and changes in the furniture reflect a new understanding of the regular acts of worship. The Victorians were often sufficiently aware of tourism to demolish the heavy stone *pulpitum* between choir and nave because they wanted to offer the excitement of a 'vista' of the whole church. But since clergy and laity must still be separated, a less bulky screen of stone, iron or wood was usually thought necessary. In recent years even this mark of separation has often been abolished in order to unite clergy and congregation using the whole church. So the Victorian screen has been thrown out (even when in a cathedral built for Roman Catholics the screen was intended to be the most prominent feature). In the centre of the cathedral – as of many a lesser church – a simple altar has been placed close to the congregation and at its level, in accordance with the emphasis of the 'liturgical' movement on the participation of the people in the service.

Modern sculpture, windows, woodwork and vestments have been introduced into the cathedrals. Sometimes the modern building material, concrete, has appeared unashamedly. The intention has been to revive the tradition of Christian art in the idiom natural to the people of today – the idiom of a society where

39

honesty is the first ideal. That has meant plain surfaces and straight lines, leaving the unadulterated material to show any beauty it can. And it has meant honest images of anxiety, doubt and suffering. The east window of **Salisbury Cathedral** presents the suffering of prisoners of conscience. In the midst of Salisbury Close – the most beautiful collection of houses and lawns in England – a statue of the Walking Madonna is a masterpiece by Dame Elizabeth Frink. But the serenity has gone. She is seeking something and on her face is etched hard experience. She leads a pilgrim people through a troubled time into an uncertain future. This sculpture is a far cry from the old image of the Queen of Heaven, just as the east window is a far cry from the medieval Church's elegant celebration of its triumph.

Naturally, these changes have caused controversy. Some would wish to preserve the cathedral's aloofness from consumerism and modern fashions and agonies, even while they welcome modern luxuries such as electric light and heat in winter. But one thing may be said with certainty. The Gothic revival which aroused so much Victorian energy has had a lasting effect in encouraging respect for the creations of the Middle Ages. Nowadays when we enter a Norman or Gothic building we want to learn and to enjoy, not to sneer. Usually we build a new church in our own style, one reason being that work in cut stone is horribly expensive now that masons are better paid than they were in the Middle Ages. But often we are uneasily aware that the job was done better in the old days.

The cathedrals of Britain are, architecturally speaking, often the poor relations of the cathedrals of France, which number about 80. But in one way this country now has the advantage. Our cathedrals attract many voluntary helpers and supporters. So far these friends have been able to maintain the cathedrals without any assistance from the State (which cold-heartedly adds a tax to the financial value of repairs). In France the cathedrals are owned by the State and this bureaucratic control has had the effect of discouraging local lay involvement, although of course not completely. The visitor accustomed to the cathedrals of Britain admires the glory but misses the flowers, the voluntary guides, the coffee, the sense of the happy amateurism of local love. In Britain only Glasgow Cathedral is the property of the Crown and the response to a long series of appeals to the public to 'save' cathedral fabrics (beginning with St Albans in 1871) has been amazingly adequate up to the end of the 1980s. The principle of free admission (established at Chester in 1926) is rightly popular and in the 1980s most of the cathedrals are maintaining it. But there has been much understanding of the financial needs which mean that gifts from visitors must be solicited and purchases by tourists must be facilitated. The staff of the cathedral must surprise themselves by learning the art and craft of salesmanship. The time may come when State aid is needed. But it is to be hoped that any arrangements will include an essential place for the affectionate loyalty of the local community.

Walking Madonna *by Elizabeth Frink brings the 20th century to Salisbury Close.*

THE
MASTER BUILDERS

6 ANGLO-SAXONS AND NORMANS

The crypt of York Minster was rebuilt under the 14th-century choir, but the Norman carved capitals of the pillars survived.

The impact of a work of art ought not to depend entirely on our knowing who did it and when. Art ought to communicate by shape, texture or colour and ought to speak directly to that part of the brain which enjoys such things without the language of words and without any knowledge of history. The art of the Middle Ages, for example, can give us pleasure or delight even if we ignore the historical background. But our understanding can be deepened by some knowledge of the society which erupts in a work of art as a volcano erupts in fire and lava. Even modern abstract art is *modern*, created within some conventions and therefore received without total incomprehension. An artist must have his own integrity but is someone's pupil, apprentice or employee, with an imagination fed by the food of the day. The general rule which applies to most of the history of art is thoroughly true of the Middle Ages and of all art in a medieval style: the artist may be a pioneer in emotion or technique but his identity is largely submerged in the identity of the society of which he is a child and a servant. When art is in the service of the Church the artist must share the faith of the patron who commissions him and of the worshippers who will live with his work. He must be an innocent believer or at least he must be willing to suspend any private disbelief, for he works not primarily in order to express himself but in order to express what the community holds to be sacred. And the community exists, even more obviously than does the artist himself, in a history with dates.

Anglo-Saxon Fragments

Little art with a Christian character survives from Roman Britain and none of it needs to be considered here − for no building known to have been a cathedral has been excavated. The earliest clear evidence of Christianity's presence in Britain comes in the decrees of a council held at Arles in the south of France in 314. This meeting was attended by Eborius Bishop of York, Restitutus Bishop of London and Adelfius Bishop of Lincoln (but the scribe wrote *Colonia Londinensium*, which seems to be a mistake for *Colonia Lindensium*). When the withdrawal of the Roman legions over the next 100 years left Britain open to pirates and invaders Christianity went more or less underground in England, although the legend of Arthur reflects the fact that some Christians put up a fight. When the West Saxons arrived in Glastonbury early in the 8th century they found that the wooden church there was in use and revered as old. More important was the spread of Christianity from a post-Roman country to Wales and to the Picts in southern Scotland. Missionaries went to Ireland and from Ireland back to Scotland and England through the holy islands of Iona and Lindisfarne. St Cuthbert died on Iona, his missionary base, in 597, eight days after the baptism in Canterbury of King Ethelbert of Kent by St Augustine, a missionary bishop sent from Rome by Pope Gregory the Great. The decision at the Synod of Whitby to accept the Roman Catholic date of Easter in 664, rather than the date customary among Celtic Christians, marked the virtual end of the Celtic form of Christianity in England. When Anglo-Saxon England became devoutly Christian, some of its customs were its own but it had a strong feeling that it did belong to the Catholic world. The spread of Roman Catholicism to Scotland, Wales and Ireland was, however, a much slower business.

Almost all Anglo-Saxon art or architecture has perished. Much of it − including embroidery and decorated books of surpassing beauty − was looted by the Normans, taken to churches on the continent and subsequently destroyed. Almost all the wooden churches were burned. The only cathedral which survives above ground, although now a ruin, is in North Elmham in Norfolk and it is less than a quarter of the size of the Norman cathedral in Norwich. The earlier timber cathedral in South Elmham in Suffolk was smaller. Churches were small because in a country with bad or no roads the population was small, perhaps two million in the whole of Britain in 1050.

However, Anglo-Saxon churches which are small can still have an impressive atmosphere and about 250 of their stone or 'white' churches have survived. At Escomb near Durham the little village church which incorporates Roman material is famous for its power to suggest Anglo-Saxon worship. A church built about 680 in the village of

Brixworth near Northampton has a touch of Roman grandeur along with some use of Roman tiles, although its aisles have gone. The monastery of Deerhurst near Gloucester survives from a date almost as ancient with crude triangular windows made by placing three stones together, but these walls are high, there is sculpture and the piety of the Saxons has also left behind, not many yards away, a memorial chapel dedicated in 1056. So E. A. Fisher's book of 1962 takes more than 400 pages to discuss *The Greater Anglo-Saxon Churches*. Probably the Anglo-Saxon cathedrals, small as they were, did not completely deserve demolition. That is suggested by the remains of Reculver Abbey now in the crypt of Canterbury, particularly by the fragments of a sculptured cross probably as old as the church in Brixworth; and rather simpler crosses are preserved in Ely and York. There is an exhibition of Anglo-Saxon work in stone in Durham. We must stop to admire the Hedda Stone, a tomb carved with apostles in Peterborough about 800, or the coffin lid in Bristol carved with the Harrowing of Hell, or the angels in Southwell and Manchester, or the roundel of Christ the King in the chapter house of Gloucester. The treasures of York Minster include the Horn of Ulph, a drinking horn made of an elephant's tusk dating from before the Norman Conquest. And there are Saxon fonts in the present cathedrals of Wells and Hereford. But how pathetic it is that our verdict depends on such fragments!

Norman Majesty

More substantial evidence about the prestige of Anglo-Saxon Christianity is provided by a strange tribute paid by the conquering Normans. At first they seem to have hoped that their massive new churches would blot out the memories of the old English saints. They soon learned otherwise. And so the saints were honoured. St Swithun's body was moved into

the new cathedral at Winchester and St Dunstan had a shrine in Canterbury's second Norman choir. Saints who had lived very close to the earth and the poor were now housed splendidly. Just as the great church of Assisi was built in honour of St Francis, very expensively inaugurating Gothic art in Italy as a tribute to a man who made a cult of total poverty, so all the attention-grabbing might of Durham Cathedral was built around the emaciated body of a hermit, St Cuthbert. And this homage to holiness says something about the Norman character.

The Normans or 'Northmen' were descendants of the Scandinavian Vikings who had so often burned down Anglo-Saxon cathedrals and monasteries and massacred their inmates. They were still pirates at heart, ruthless towards each other, oppressive to the conquered, but with a rare standard of courage and an even more unusual power to organise. William the Conqueror's 'harrying of the North' – a devastation punishing an attempt to rebel – was matched by the Normans' sack of Rome and by their behaviour as crusaders in the Holy Land. Yet the discipline which they imposed made later unity and progress possible and they were in their own rough way patrons of the clergy, and of artists and of scholars. Sicily under the Normans was a meeting place with the higher civilisation of the Arabs. Southern Italy was sprinkled with Norman churches and in the cathedral of Salerno one can feel something of a link with Durham. As much of Britain as they could grab was reorganised as a part of the Catholic Church of the West.

In religion the Normans combined two habits: they disregarded the Sermon on the Mount and they worshipped Almighty God. Rollo, a Norwegian pirate chief, was baptised in 1011 as a condition of being allowed to settle in France. It was the same condition that Alfred had imposed on the Danish general in 878, beginning the rapid conversion of England's resident Vikings. The Normans now regarded themselves as soldiers of Christ. In particular they admired monks, who had given up sex and private property in order to storm the gates of heaven and (it was hoped) to bring with them, by their prayers, fellow-Normans who could not renounce so much. They also admired the aura of sanctity which surrounded a bishop and although they knew that many of their bishops were in fact worldly men they trusted them more than they trusted each other. At the same time they made sure that bishops and monks did not contract out of military necessities entirely. The cement of the Norman society was the feudal system, which meant (at least in theory) that the duke-king owned all the land and could rely on the services of knights provided by his chief

A Saxon cross in York Minster.

The north transept of Peterborough shows how in the 12th century more decoration was incorporated into the Norman style.

The 12th-century font in Winchester.

tenants or 'vassals', who in their turn could rely on 'homage' and help from their tenants. A bishop or abbot who was granted estates had to produce knights just like any lay baron; and it was not unusual for him to lend a hand himself in the fighting. St Anselm, a great theologian and archbishop, worked out an explanation of the work of Christ in these feudal terms: God the Son satisfied the justice of God the supreme Overlord, to whom man had failed to give due homage.

William the Conqueror's invasion in 1066, with about 6,000 men, carried a banner which, it was claimed, conveyed the blessing of the Pope. Later, prayers and more solid gestures of 'penance' were made on the orders of the Pope's envoys in order to compensate God for the English who had been killed or robbed and in order to make sure of a blessing on the continuing colonial rule and wealth. Battle Abbey was built on the site of the battle of Hastings and the construction of about 30 other cathedrals or great monastic churches was begun in the 30 years between 1070 and 1100. Their number and size can never be other than amazing, for these churches were certainly not built in order to hold large congregations, yet the phenomenon can be explained. It is instructive to compare these churches with the two abbeys, for men and women, built in Caen in 1062-64 by the Conqueror and his queen when the former (a bastard) had been allowed to marry the latter (a woman too closely related to him by blood according to the Church's law). It is even more instructive to compare this church-building with the castle-building which no doubt interested the top Normans much more and which successfully competed with cathedrals for the labour of masons. More than 50 permanent castles were constructed in England in the years 1066-86.

A big new church in England was the most public statement of the Norman Conquest's legitimacy that could be imagined. Cathedrals in particular announced unanswerably the arrival of bishops and abbots from France – for only one Englishman was made a bishop between 1070 and 1140. The Romanesque architectural style had been picked up by the ex-pirates in Normandy because it was the style which had already been used in the 'Holy Roman' empires of Charlemagne and his successors. It had an impressive continuity with the surviving monuments of the Roman empire itself. (The Roman writer on architecture, Vitruvius, was consulted as an authority throughout the Middle Ages.) So from the first duke, Rollo, onwards those Normans who had managed to come out on top amid frequent civil wars had displayed their power in Roman-looking building projects. In conquered England such buildings could be financed out of the estates which the King granted to the senior clergy, who were less likely to rebel than the lay barons, or out of lands which these warlords granted to churchmen in exchange for promised and much-needed prayers. And under the supervision of Norman master masons the churches could be built by mostly unskilled labour, conscripted and paid a pittance. The walls would probably stand because so much stone or rubble was piled up. It did not greatly matter if some towers fell, for England provided plenty of building material and plenty of labour.

Religion and politics were mixed up inextricably in the Norman cathedral. But it is only right to add that the Norman development of the Romanesque style in architecture might well have influenced England without a conquest, since Anglo-Saxon buildings already contained features which can be called Romanesque and Anglo-Saxon masons must have contributed to buildings which are called Norman. It is instructive to consider the first Westminster Abbey. Built by King Edward the Confessor, who had spent his boyhood in Normandy, it was consecrated in 1065 a week before his death in the adjacent palace. The tapestry made for the cathedral at Bayeux in Normandy (probably by English needle-women) in celebration of the Conquest shows this church with west towers still being built. An elaborate central tower rises over transepts and in the nave are five large, rounded arches. This Westminster Abbey looks very Norman – not surprisingly, for it was modelled on the big churches attached to royal and ducal palaces in France.

At first the Norman conquerors built as plentifully, as colossally and as quickly as possible. Their early churches in England included no substantial departure from their practices in Normandy apart from the building of crypts, for which French precedents are only found in Burgundy. These churches, however, were not as gloomy as we are often inclined to think when we see what remains. Many parts of the walls were originally painted; many altars sparkled; many vestments gleamed. And after that hectic first period, the masons felt able to take time to carve decoration – at first with axes – and to experiment with stone vaulting and pointed arches. Such arches were decorative but also useful in absorbing the weight of a stone vault. Variety was possible in the design of the long naves: in Gloucester the lower arches are much taller than the triforium, in Southwell they are shorter, in Norwich they are the same size. Peterborough Cathedral, rebuilt after 1118, is much more advanced than what remains of the early Norman work in St Albans. It was thought right to preserve the beauty of decorated Norman towers at some trouble when the cathedrals of Canterbury, Exeter and Gloucester were rebuilt in more modern styles. The whole architecture of Kelso Abbey in Roxburghshire, built late in the 12th century, or the grand Norman tower of Tewkesbury Abbey, could have honoured any cathedral in any period. Among the Norman cathedrals Durham is always praised, but its awesomeness is not unique. In his volume in the *Oxford History of English Art* (1953) T. S. R. Boase wrote: 'In the twelfth century, in architecture and painting, England is a great, at moments supreme, exponent of a European style: in scale her works are indeed in the grand manner and in quality the clear product of genius'.

A Transition

The development of architecture from the purely Norman or Romanesque majesty into the confusion referred to as the 'Transitional' style can be seen in the cathedrals of Oxford and Rochester.

The church which is now the cathedral of **Oxford** was begun in the same period as the university, the 1170s or thereabouts. It was, however, not a part of the university until the 16th century. The church was an Augustinian priory and what remains of its Norman architecture is of no great beauty. Instead of the triforium being a storey in the wall, it is tucked under the big arch, with a clumsy second arch beneath it. This arrangement is seen in some other churches in the Transitional style, but it is not successful. Much more gracious is the Early English architecture added in the 13th and 14th centuries: the tower with its little spire, the three chapels beside the choir and the chapter house with its little cloister. These additions were made possible by the offerings brought to the shrine of St Frideswide, who was reputed to have founded an Anglo-Saxon nunnery here.

Cathedrals were built at **Rochester** because the spot was so strategic; this was where Watling Street, the Roman road between London and Dover, crossed the navigable estuary of the Medway. The first Rochester Cathedral was provided by the first Christian king in England, Ethelbert, for Justus, a companion of Augustine, the first Archbishop of Canterbury. Here Paulinus fled and was buried, having had to retreat from his time in the north as the first Archbishop of York. But when the Normans arrived they found the old cathedral in very poor shape and demolished it. Although Rochester remained the smallest and poorest diocese in medieval England, it was now given a cathedral monastery not unfit to stand beside the castle. The first builder

(about 1080) was Bishop Gandulf, a monk who specialised in the supervision of building projects. He was responsible for the White Tower built for the Conqueror as a castle in London (the 'Tower of London') and for Rochester Castle itself. The only parts of his cathedral which survive, however, are the detached tower (originally a fortification, it seems), a crypt and some of the nave. The nave which we see was built by one of his successors in the bishopric, Ernulf (about 1120), after a fire. It is austere. The light which now floods in – and which Charles Dickens celebrated in his unfinished last novel, *Edwin Drood* – comes through later, Perpendicular, windows. But the round Norman arches are decorated and the gallery above them strangely has no floor, as if preparing for the Early English presbytery where the triforium is completely abolished in favour of a taller clerestory.

In 1160-75 the west front was remodelled to include turrets at both ends, and around the central doorway a 'portal' of sculptures was crowned by Christ in Majesty. The weather has almost destroyed the carving but it does not seem completely ridiculous to remember in Rochester the majestic sculptures of Chartres. Within England, one can get some idea of what this portal looked like originally by admiring the sculptures of apostles and angels inside the porch of the half-ruined Norman abbey in Malmesbury.

7 THE GOTHIC REVOLUTION

The change from Norman through Transitional into the lightness, pointedness and simplicity of Early English began the full 'Gothic' style. It was a major revolution in the history of architecture. The decisive moment was the rebuilding of the choir of Canterbury from 1175, made possible by the wealth already being brought by pilgrims to the tomb of the recently martyred Thomas Becket. The monks of Rochester, always with their eyes on Canterbury, must have been ineffectively jealous until one of these pilgrims, William, a baker from Perth, was murdered in their own little city during 1201. They seized their chance to establish his shrine as a pilgrimage centre. The pilgrims would make a noise (so that before long the monks were building a wall around the place where they sang their services). But they would also bring money and gleefully the monks – or, rather, their masons – built a graceful Early English east end surrounding their high altar and St William. Here the abolition of the triforium makes for a much lighter atmosphere, and shafts of Purbeck marble rise from floor to vault. Later the monks could afford to work westwards, modernizing the transepts and part of the nave under a new tower, but pilgrimages to St William dried up and Rochester's architectural ambitions had to be ended.

The change from Transitional to Early English was not made overnight. Norman work which had been begun was completed in the same style (as in Peterborough). In the nave of York huge arches which were scarcely pointed were still thought sufficiently fashionable at the end of the 13th century. In Wales and Scotland the new pointed fashion was ignored or resisted for many years (as it was in more prosperous Germany). In addition to conservatism, political uncertainty was a discouraging factor in England. After the death of Henry I there was civil war between the supporters of Stephen and Matilda and after the death of Henry II the throne was occupied first by Richard, a lion-hearted absentee, and then by John, who quarrelled first with the papacy and then with the barons. But the 100 years between 1150 and 1250 formed a creative age for architecture as the countryside was covered by thousands of new parish churches and the new Cistercian movement built a

number of large monasteries, deliberately both simple and lovely. That was the background to the creation after about 1190 of the glorious cathedrals of Lincoln, Wells and Salisbury, which seem to be jumping up and down for joy.

Glasgow Cathedral can be mentioned in the same breath, although it would be tactless to call its style Early English. The crypt and choir of the present church were built mainly in the first half of the 13th century; the nave was rebuilt a century later and the whole building had to be thoroughly restored by the Victorians. To the medieval Scots the centre of interest was in the dark but beautifully carved crypt, for here was the shrine of St Kentigern (also called St Mungo), who brought the Gospel to this region in the 6th century. After the Reformation the great church, with its spire on a steeply sloping hill, escaped the Scottish cathedral's normal fate of rooflessness and ruin.

What lay behind this architectural revolution? The psychological answer is that the high Middle Ages were beginning. The years 1214-15 were in many ways a turning point. These are the years when King John lost Normandy and sealed Magna Carta; henceforth England was going to be a nation on its own and one which would never give unbridled power to its king. But the backing of King John by the Papacy was a symptom of new vitality and power in the Church. The Lateran Council in Rome issued many decrees which ordered the laity to confess their sins to a priest at least once a year and which determined the life of the medieval Church with an ordered clarity seen also in the new theology of the universities. A new age was in the air around the new buildings. However, if we are to answer our question in the terms of architecture we have to admit that England and Scotland were influenced by a richer country, France.

About 1135 Abbot Suger decided to rebuild his church of **St Denis** near Paris. This church's function as the guardian of the shrine of a popular saint made it important to provide easier access and more space for the pilgrims – and its function as the guardian of royal tombs made it possible to finance the work from rich endowments. The abbot himself, a peasant's son, was virtually Prime Minister of France – although that modern title is even more than

The choir of Canterbury proclaimed the Gothic revolution to England. William the Englishman took over from William of Sens as master mason in 1182.

usually inappropriate, for in this period the French monarchy still had to assert itself against overmighty barons. The region around Paris (the Île de France) was the scene of royal patronage of new churches which would advertise the monarchy and its piety. But Suger's plan for his church reflected more than political aims. He was conscious of living in a time when Christian scholars were beginning to think with new courage. It was the age of Abelard, who taught students to question the authority of those ancient theologians, the Fathers of the Church. The medieval theological movement which we call Scholasticism, operating under the influence of the Greek philosophy of Plato and Aristotle and culminating in the work of St Thomas Aquinas, was being born. Suger took seriously the current mystical thinking that dwelt on the sacredness of light. He also took seriously the protests of reforming churchmen such as St Bernard of Clairvaux against the decoration of churches with fantastic and non-Christian subjects (such as the beasts who fight in the crypt of Canterbury Cathedral). He wanted a Christian logic in stone.

So the St Denis which Suger rebuilt – and which he explained in books intended to spread his architectural ideas, the first of their kind in Christian Europe – was like many other churches a mixture of political propaganda and sincere religion. Its essential structure can still be seen although there have been many later additions and many of the treasures which enthused the medieval pilgrims have disappeared. The west front consisted of three large inviting doorways with fine carvings of biblical subjects around them and a 'rose' window above them. Inside, the church was flooded with coloured light from tall windows in nine new chapels. A spacious passage leading round the shrine (an ambulatory) further transformed the experience of the pilgrims. In it, pointed arches led the eye upwards to ribbed vaults and beyond them perhaps to thoughts of heaven. Other great churches in France were adopting some of these novelties in the same period, but it was Suger's work in St Denis, consecrated in 1144, that gave them the publicity which eventually influenced England. So it has usually been reckoned that this is the place where the Gothic style began.

In France the Gothic cathedrals sprang up: Laon, the vast church of Notre Dame in Paris, Chartres, Rheims, Amiens, Bourges . . . Among these it was Rheims Cathedral, where the French kings were crowned, that largely inspired the next revolution in English church architecture. In the choir at Rheims, which was rebuilt between 1211 and 1241, windows were for the first time divided by stone tracery. This development and the contemporary building of the Sainte Chapelle in Paris fulfilled the vision of a church as a stone-and-glass introduction to heaven.

King Henry III, a genuinely interested patron of the Church and the arts, determined to build (out of taxation) a similar church, where all his successors on the throne of England were to be consecrated and crowned and where he and many of them were to buried. To do this he pulled down the eastern half of **Westminster Abbey** in 1245, consoling King Edward the Confessor, now canonized as a saint, by a sumptuous new shrine. The new abbey had a height never before seen in England – over 30 metres (100 feet) – the vault being supported by 'flying' buttresses of unprecedented size. It introduced the art of tracery in large windows, including rose windows in the transepts. On the thin walls royally rich decoration was carved and painted. The carving of four 'censing angels' in the south transept was the most beautiful sculpture ever executed in medieval England (so far as we know), competing with the smiling angels of Rheims. From the west fronts of Rheims and Amiens was derived the splendid north front, intended as the state entrance, and Rheims also suggested the five chapels radiating out of the ambulatory round the choir. The personal history of the master mason, Henry de Reyns, is not known (see page 17), but his name suggests that he was summoned to Westminster from work in Rheims. His architectural nervousness is betrayed by the abundance of wooden and iron ties, added to give stability to what were in England experiments.

The design of Westminster Abbey was never exactly reproduced in England, although there is an echo of it in Hereford Cathedral. Cost was the decisive deterrent when there was no Henry III to divert a kingdom's revenue into ecclesiastical architecture. In Westminster itself work on the nave in approximately the same style was not begun until 1376 and was not completed until 1502. The building of the west towers had to wait until 1745 and the central tower never has been built. But another reason for Westminster's uniqueness was English conservatism. The English suspected the Frenchified novelties introduced by a Frenchified king. They adopted some of them but were never willing to abandon totally their national and regional traditions.

What Westminster Abbey did for English architecture was to encourage some experiments in ornamenting the basically traditional style. The failure to copy France thoroughly is often lamented by those who regard the French cathedral as the crown of the Middle Ages. In his survey of international *Gothic Architecture* (1986) Louis Grodecki complained that too

often in England 'a readable structure was sacrificed for the sake of decorative interests that have little to do with logical clarity. . . . Of all French influences operating at Westminster, English architects retained only two essential features: broadening and lengthening of the windows and a new ornamental imaginativeness evolving from intricate window tracery'. More flatteringly, Peter Brieger asserted in his volume in the *Oxford History of English Art* (1957) that 'English builders found their own manner of achieving lightness and light, articulate flexibility and elastic firmness without reaching as high towards heaven and without sacrificing the appearance of common sense stability'.

When greatness was wanted, as it was when the nave of York Minster was rebuilt between 1291 and 1346, it was believed that it could be achieved by reproducing a conservative style on a very big scale. York's height, almost that of Westminster's, was matched by breadth – so that in the end it was not possible to cover the vault in stone. And greatness was achieved in Wells Cathedral, in a permanent exhibition of sculpture that was precisely a conservative and decorative celebration of the English Christian heritage. The statues put on the west front of Wells, wrote Peter Brieger, 'lack the emotional tension and the personal expressions of earlier and later periods, but their faces shine with physical beauty, keen intelligence and humane benevolence, not to be found again until the time of the High Renaissance'.

8 DECORATED SPLENDOUR

A capital in the chapter house of Southwell displays vine leaves and grapes carved in the 1290s.

It is not always obvious now why the next great style in church architecture is called Decorated. The ornamentation carved in stone in medieval churches – for example, the 'ball-flowers' which could be scattered lest a space be left plain – has lost much of its purpose now that the paint on it has almost entirely disappeared. But Melrose Abbey and Roslin Chapel near Edinburgh are splendid examples of decorated architecture in Scotland and in its cathedrals England can also exhibit some spectacular examples of showmanship in stone carving during this exuberantly confident period. We marvel at the Salisbury spire, the 'palm tree' which forms the central pillar of the chapter house in Wells, the Neville screen above the high altar in Durham, the naves of York, Exeter and Lichfield, the two choirs of Lincoln and those two miracles in Ely: the octagon which pours light into the middle of the cathedral and the Lady chapel which although vandalized is still full of grace. Some of the Decorated showmanship, we ought to admit, was a failure. In Hereford triangular arches from the 'geometric' period eliminated all Westminster's curves, and later, in many more places, 'ogee' arches indulged in double curves; and neither style is as beautiful as its simpler predecessors and successors. Not all the other architectural experiments – in Lincoln Cathedral, for example – ended up being beautiful. But the small cathedral of **Bristol** provides examples of the courage which experimented with success. We have to congratulate an architect whose name is unknown.

Before it was made a cathedral in 1542 this church had almost exactly 400 years of life as an abbey of Augustinian canons, on a little hill a few yards away from the river where seagoing ships unloaded their goods. Eventually Bristol became a centre of the Atlantic trade and already in the Middle Ages it may have stimulated the citizens, including the clergy, into becoming patrons of up-to-date architecture. The willingness to be new can certainly be seen in the porch of St Mary Redcliffe, which has always been the leading merchants' favourite church. But it can also be seen in the cathedral. The oldest substantial building is the chapter house, built about 1150. The tracery on the north and south walls is a vigorous example of inventive energy in various abstract designs, poured out in an earlier transition, from Norman to Early English, but the pointed arch is only one among a number of motifs. The older of the two Lady chapels, built between 40 and 60 years after the chapter house, shows the more playful mood of Early English. There is foliage in this carving and animals have fun in the 'spandrels' above the arches. The abbot of the time borrowed at least one stonemason from the Dean of Wells, where the new nave was exhibiting this style on a larger scale.

Abbot Knowle, who ruled from 1306 to 1332, was far more adventurous than his predecessor. He gave his architect a free hand despite startling innovations. The use of lierne (decorative, not functional) ribs in the vaults was not a complete novelty; in addition to the experiments of Geoffrey de Noiers in Lincoln, such ribs had been used in St Stephen's Chapel in Westminster and in Pershore Abbey. But in Bristol these ribs created a new beauty, in which the whole vault is seen as one entity instead of the eye taking it in bay by bay. Another novelty was the use of 'flying' ribs in the vault of the Berkeley Chapel; the only comparable experiments of approximately the same date are on a smaller scale, in the Easter Sepulchre and the *pulpitum* at Lincoln and in the *pulpitum* at Southwell. Another and more ambitious experiment was to make the aisles the same height as the broad vault, which was supported by struts and arches ingeniously functioning as buttresses. Although such hall churches were not unknown in continental Europe (Poitiers Cathedral had been begun in this style in the 1160s), and in England small parts of churches had been made in this way (for example, the eastern chapel of Salisbury Cathedral), Bristol's nearest English precedents had been in the halls of lords and bishops. This particular experiment was not repeated, although it was not the end of architectural inventiveness in Bristol, as the cathedral's curious star-shaped tomb recesses testify.

Since the great rose window which so impressed medieval London above the high altar of Old St Paul's is no more, we find the finest surviving examples of the Decorated window in Lincoln's Angel Choir and transepts, and in York at both ends of the Minster. As we

admire them we shall certainly understand why this style of tracery in window-building is called 'geometric' before it becomes 'curvilinear'. But here we may concentrate on a window which has survived many hazards to be the most admired feature of a much battered cathedral, **Carlisle**.

Carlisle is a frontier town. The present border with Scotland is only seven miles away, and remnants of Hadrian's Wall are found in the outskirts of the city and also, it is said, in the cathedral itself, explaining why some dark grey stones are mixed with the coral red sandstone. Centuries of bitter war between England and Scotland marked the history and fabric of this church. It was made a cathedral in 1133 by Henry I, patron of the Augustinian canons whom he brought to Carlisle not long after their introduction into England. Carlisle had then been in English hands for less than 40 years and had remained in the diocese of Glasgow. A little over 500 years later, Scots troops who had temporarily seized the town back pulled down three quarters of the nave in order to make fortifications. The nave has never been rebuilt. What remained of the fabric of the cathedral deteriorated, as sandstone always does, and had to be rescued by the Victorians (with Euan Christian as architect). But despite these dangers and disasters, Carlisle Cathedral has preserved some good furnishings, most notably the canons' stalls from about 1425. Lancelot Salkeld, the last prior who became the first dean in 1542, gave a fine screen of Renaissance design. Expelled as a Catholic under Edward VI, restored under Mary and expelled again under Elizabeth, his screen nevertheless remains. The older wooden barrel vault in the chancel has recently been painted with stars and sky. And at the east end is the glorious window of about 1370 with five lights, 15.5 metres (51 feet) tall. The middle light expands at the top into tracery of a rare loveliness. This delicate stonework still holds some of the original glass although the glass below is Victorian, by John Hardman.

The constant temptation of Decorated to become Overdecorated can be seen clearly in **Southwell Minster**, made a cathedral for Nottinghamshire in 1884. The chief glory is the carving in the chapter house – an important room because in the Middle Ages almost 50 clergy were entitled to sit here, with a palace for the Archbishop of York next door. (This college of canons, without a dean, survived until 1840 and all the best houses in this lovely little town were built for its lucky members.) The carving's contribution to the enchanting beauty of the chapter house, a contribution strictly confined to the right places, can be seen all the better because this smallish room has never had a central pillar and now has

mostly clear glass in its large windows. We owe this glory to at least three sculptors in the 1290s. They showed how well they could make lifelike human heads and carve little animals too, but they preferred leaves of oak, maple, hawthorn, ivy, rose, vine, buttercup and hop. Each is recreated with an exact perception of a leaf and of how it differs from stone, in a radical departure from the tradition of unrecognizable 'stiff leaf'. The cutting in this buff gritstone is extraordinarily crisp and deep. It was never painted; it did not need paint. It has never been 'restored'; its craftsmanship could never be matched. If we compare it with the Norman sculpture in the Canterbury crypt we see that it is the work of men who no longer had nightmares about beasts fighting each other. The battle of faith had been won. As Sir Nikolaus Pevsner wrote in his deeply felt little book on *The Leaves of Southwell* (1945) which was read at his memorial service, this celebration was inspired by 'the conviction that so much beauty can exist only because God is in every man and beast, in every herb and stone'.

Elsewhere in Southwell Minster there is much good architecture to be enjoyed. A Saxon church was built on the site of a Roman villa; a Norman church replaced it, and its west front survives (although restored) to advertise its plain dignity; the more ornamented Norman towers also survive; in the nave the three storeys are slightly stepped, so that they expand outwards as they go up; the large triforium is windowless, adding to the air of cavernous mystery; the chancel is elegantly Early English. The eye has a feast of treats. But the *pulpitum* can be called Overdecorated. It has spaces for altars beneath its three arches, and its lavish carving includes about 220 little human heads with much flat and formal foliage. It represents a decline from the creation of the perfect leaves of the chapter house.

In **Newcastle upon Tyne** between 1450 and 1475, the new tower was crowned by a bit of Decorated flamboyance – four flying buttresses which are pinnacled and which (after a number of restorations) still hold up a small spire. The tower is at least 20 years older than the similar steeple which crowns St Giles Cathedral in Edinburgh. A considerable number of lesser statements of civic pride may be found inside this parish church of St Nicholas, which was not made a cathedral until 1882, for there is a rich collection of memorials. When the Norman church had been destroyed by fire in about 1225 the citizens rebuilt, and they built again in the next century on a larger scale (although without any capitals on the piers). But the only impact of the Decorated style within the church is on some windows and on the elaborate canopy over the font, of about 1500. It is the tower that announces that Newcastle is the centre of an important region and is not to be confused with Durham. The touch of flamboyance is a hint of what might have developed in Britain, although it is modest when compared with the extravaganzas to be seen in continental Europe. Nothing in Britain competes with the ornamented vastness of the cathedrals of Milan and Seville, or the exuberance of *Sondergotik* in Germany, or the frenzy of the west front of Rouen.

9 THE PERPENDICULAR STYLE

Instead of more flamboyance, England developed a style which has more claim than 'Early English' to be called its own. In the Middle Ages continental architects had no wish to copy such architecture and in modern times continental experts have not been very willing to admire it. The Gothic revival in Victorian Britain did not often revert to it. John Ruskin taught the Victorians to prefer the 15th century in Venice and they welcomed the lesson because they loved decoration. But here is an English beauty. The Perpendicular style combines the discipline of restraint with the impact of simplicity. It unites elegance with economy.

In 1327 Edward II was murdered on the orders of his queen and her lover. The aristocracy accepted the event calmly, as it was to accept the probable murders of Richard II and Henry VI in an age when a king's most admired role was leadership in military conquest. Edward was a patron of handsome and arrogant young men; Richard, although a devoted husband, was a patron of artists and himself an aesthete; Henry was virtually a monk. None of them impressed their subjects in comparison with Edward II's father who conquered Wales and Scotland, or his son who conquered France. However, the murder of a crowned and anointed king aroused popular feelings. Even the execution of Thomas, Earl of Lancaster, after a rebellion against Edward II, had produced a cult; he was remembered not as the nasty man he had been but as a martyr for Church and People. Now King Edward himself could be said to be a martyr of some sort and an opportunity arose for an enterprising church to make his tomb a shrine. The opportunity was seized by the abbot of **Gloucester.** The largest contribution to the project came from a government anxious to prove the respectability of the new reign, but offerings from pilgrims helped. The modernization of the east arm of this great monastic church could now be financed.

The work in the transepts (in the 1330s) and the rest of the east arm (in the 1350s and 60s) was done in a new style which had been tried out by the King's own master mason, William Ramsey, in St Stephen's chapel in the palace of Westminster and in the chapter house of St Paul's Cathedral in London. Royal masons superintended the changes in Gloucester which publicized the 'Perpendicular' style on a new scale. Slender columns now climbed without interruption from floor to vault. Mullions now rose more or less straight to the top of windows; the windows in the clerestory were tall enough to pour in light; the east window which replaced the rounded stone apse, filled with glass which also let in light, was at that time the world's largest. And tracery was no longer confined to the windows. It filled the stone screens which now masked the clumsier Norman work, like a new skin for the church. In this panelling on the walls patterns were plain and 'rectilinear', almost right-angled, replacing the curves and complicated cleverness of the Decorated style. It was an architecture of unity, of totality, like the Norman style, only infinitely more sophisticated. Its restraint was courtly, the restraint of good taste.

In the cloister, which seems to have been designed by Thomas of Cambridge in the 1350s, a new style of vaulting was developed – fan vaulting. Above windows filled with glass, large blocks of stone on which fan-like tracery had already been carved bulged out and were locked by circles into other bulges, looking a

The Perpendicular retrochoir of Peterborough was designed by John Wastell about 1500.

Monks' studies beneath the fan vaulting of Gloucester Cathedral's cloister.

bit like umbrellas or ice cream cones. Each square vaulted in this way in the cloister was fairly small and within the cathedral the new vaulting of the choir was far more traditional – a wonderful mesh of liernes and tiercerons with musical angels providing the bosses. But when later masons developed the new technique so that large rectangular spaces could be fan-vaulted (now using ribs and adding stone infilling between them), people saw that this new treatment of a vault brilliantly matched the rest of the Perpendicular style.

Here was a style originally designed for elegance rather than economy, but during the modernization of Gloucester, in 1348-49, the Black Death struck as the first of a number of epidemics. Skilled labour became scarcer and therefore more expensive. It was thanks to the simplicity of the stone carving in the new style that it became possible to modernize or build churches during the next 200 years on a sustainable budget. We can understand why the style is sometimes called 'Businessman's Gothic' or despised as medieval mass production, but these economies in money and skill were compatible with a great achievement in 1350-1530. This was a time of many calamities, yet the continuity of English art was not interrupted. When the English were thrown out of France (in the Hundred Years' War) and then convulsed by civil wars (the Wars of the Roses), there was a temporary stagnation or degeneration in some art – but even then beauty was still being made in England. And the Middle Ages ended with a burst of rich creativity when peace was imposed by the victorious Yorkist, Edward IV, during the 1470s, and secured in the early Tudor years.

As the masons gained the confidence needed to work on a larger scale, the repetition which was a part of this style became sumptuous in the Perpendicular walls of the naves of Canterbury and Winchester and in the vault of **King's College Chapel** in Cambridge. This extraordinary chapel was planned in the 1440s with the dimensions of a cathedral for the devotions of 70 scholars, and entrusted by its patron Henry VI to the master mason Reginald of Ely. It was completed at the expense of Henry VII between 1508 and 1515 with John Wastell as master mason. The fan vault which runs from end to end is lavishly spread but basically simple in comparison with the richer vaulting commissioned by Edward IV for St George's Chapel in Windsor (almost a cathedral of chivalry) and by Henry VII for the chapel around his own tomb in Westminster Abbey (almost a cathedral of royalism). The fan vault in Cambridge creates its unique effect because it is suspended over walls that are almost literally walls of coloured glass.

The vault of that Cambridge chapel also contrasts with the shorter but richer vault over the choir of what is now the cathedral in **Oxford**. This was constructed about 1500, immediately before Henry VII's chapel in Westminster. The tracery on both sides is straightforward Perpendicular, but in the centre is a series of squares intricately adorned with liernes and pendants. The carving was supervised by William Orchard, who had recently made a similarly prodigious vault for the Divinity Schools in Oxford. It seems that Cardinal Wolsey intended to pull it down some 30 years after its completion, together with the rest of the church, since he had designed another chapel for the Cardinal College he was creating. Before his own fall he did destroy almost half the cloister and all but three bays of the nave. Henry VIII, however, on taking over all Wolsey's many buildings, preserved what remained. He made this church the chapel of a college (Christ Church) in 1529 and the cathedral of a diocese (England's smallest cathedral) in 1542.

In the late Middle Ages English masons were commissioned for many projects in addition to the splendour accorded to dead or alive kings, their guests in Windsor and their scholars in Cambridge and Oxford. It was a time when many additions were being made to the quieter beauty in the parish churches, especially in parishes where wealth was derived from the trade in wool and cloth. It was also a time when people wanted more privacy and even comfort in their lives. In large churches such as cathedrals a stone screen or *pulpitum* was often built between choir and nave, protecting the clergy from some of the noise and the cold. And it was a time of new aspirations, held all the more keenly because of the disasters in foreign and domestic wars. Tower-building in the parishes was permanently changing the English landscape, and Perpendicular towers for cathedrals, beginning at Worcester, pulled the sprawling length of the English great church together and up. We might almost call these towers skyscrapers. In towers great or small which were belfries the peculiarly English art of change ringing was begun in the 15th century although it did not become widely popular until the 17th and the first 'peal' (of at least 5,000 'changes') was not rung until 1715. The Church's law required only one bell to summon worshippers; in continental Europe where more bells were rung they made a clangour; but in England a 'ring' (of at least five bells) had to be disciplined like the tower's architecture.

The late Middle Ages were also a time of new aspirations of and for women and a new intensity of devotion was being paid to the mother of Jesus. In Gloucester, for example,

The Perpendicular Lady chapel of Gloucester, built in the late 15th century, is entered under a bridge which carries a chantry chapel.

the Coronation of the Virgin was depicted in the great east window and an exquisitely lovely Lady chapel was built beyond it (1457-98). The 'assumption' of the Virgin – her escape from death – was often the subject of windows elsewhere. Statues of her showed on her face a radiant, triumphant, all-embracing love which was more than mortal.

When Eleanor, the queen of Edward I, died near Lincoln in 1290 the line of a dozen Eleanor Crosses along the route of her body to burial in Westminster was the spectacular beginning of a new concentration on monuments to women and men who had died. Thousands of brasses commemorated the more distinguished of the deceased on the floors of English churches, and the effigies on the tombs began to resemble portraits more closely. Names began to appear on tombs after about 1400, although very hesitantly. Flattery was not the only motive. It became the fashion for a man who had been mighty in his lifetime – for example, a bishop – to order that beneath the effigy of himself robed in all dignity of his office should be another recumbent statue, of a decomposing corpse. Bishop Fleming, who founded Lincoln College in Oxford, is thus commemorated in Lincoln Cathedral. Archbishop Chichele, who founded All Souls College, Oxford is similarly shown in Canterbury Cathedral. In Winchester little creatures are shown using Bishop Foxe's body as food. But the most elaborate monuments were little churches within the churches – the 'chantry' chapels where Mass would be said for the souls of the benefactor and his family until the end of time. Bishops built such chapels in their cathedrals, usually while they were alive and able to make sure that they got what they wanted, as we can see in Winchester or Ely. The chantry chapel of Henry, Duke of Gloucester, in St Albans, is as noble as that of his brother, Henry V, in Westminster Abbey. In Lincoln Cathedral the first chantry chapel was built in 1235 and the last in 1542, the very year when Parliament forbade its use.

No medieval cathedral was built completely in the Perpendicular style; it is a great gap. But we do have **Bath Abbey**, which has always had a special association with Wells Cathedral in the diocese of Bath and Wells. A monastery was built next to the abandoned Roman baths in 676, and rebuilt when in the 1090s a Norman bishop tried to make it Somerset's cathedral. After the defeat of this attempt the monastery fell into decay until a much later bishop, Oliver King, decided to pull everything down and start again. The new church, begun in 1499, was about half the size of the old and the King's master masons, the brothers Robert and William Vertue, turned their attention from the glories of Windsor and Westminster to work on it. Making the transepts and aisles narrow, they intended to create a roomful of light. That impression is still conveyed although most of the church we see is not medieval. It was incomplete when the monks were expelled in 1539. The nave then stood roofless until a plastered ceiling was put up in the 17th century. That satisfied the residents of Bath when it became a spa in the 18th century, although the many monuments around the walls suggest that they were neither unaware of style nor stricken by poverty. Eventually in the 1860s the chancel's fan vault was continued over the nave by Sir George Gilbert Scott. Stained glass was added to the tall windows. At last Bath Abbey was elegant.

The present **Manchester Cathedral** was built in the Perpendicular style although it was not made a cathedral until 1847. Its sandstone needed, and received, a thorough Victorian restoration. Since then there have been additions (the west porch and spacious vestries); the devastation wrought by a land-mine in 1940 has been made good; the industrial grime has been cleaned off the exterior; and the church has been enriched by modern art, including windows since none of the old glass survived the Second World War.

The cathedral is a large church not because Manchester's population was large before modern industry arrived but because of a rector who stood in a line of clergy going back to Anglo-Saxon days. Thomas de la Warr was also lord of the manor and he had the vision of a church in which a college of priests under a warden would pray for the souls of benefactors, including himself. Licensed by Henry V in 1421, his scheme attracted rich endowments. The chantry chapels made the church England's widest – 35 metres (114 feet) – and a superb angel roof spanned choir and nave. The fifth warden (1485-1509) was James Stanley. Because his father became Earl of Derby after decisively helping Henry VII to win the battle of Bosworth Field James Stanley was given the lush bishopric of Ely, but he chose to be buried in Manchester. To this church he presented 27 priests' stalls, probably the work of the Ripon master carpenter William Brownfleet, and a wood screen; all these still survive. Some of the chantry chapels used by the priests also survive (although James Stanley's own chantry chapel was not rebuilt after the blitz), and so, amazingly, do the priests' houses, originally Thomas da la Warr's manor house. They have been used as a school since 1653, most recently for the education of young musicians.

10 THE GOTHIC REVIVAL

We speak of the 'Gothic revival' because before this movement gathered force there was so much destruction of the legacy of the Middle Ages.

The survival intact of Beverley Minster and Selby Abbey – those marvellous, cathedral-like buildings which now serve Yorkshire towns as parish churches – was not typical. It has been reckoned that there were more than 700 great churches in medieval England and Wales and that nine tenths of them were destroyed, either in whole or in part, or allowed to go into ruin like Fountains, Rievaulx, Tintern or Glastonbury Abbey, when the fervour of the Reformation overthrew the religion which had inspired their construction. Of the vast abbey of Bury St Edmunds, which had been the chief landmark and landlord of Suffolk, two gateways remained; of the grandeur of Waltham Abbey in Essex, only the Norman nave and the Lady Chapel; of rich Evesham Abbey, only a gateway and a superb bell tower (built in the 1530s!); of Iona Abbey, founded by St Columba in 563, largely rebuilt in the 15th century, ruins neglected until the 1870s; of Lindisfarne Priory on the Holy Island, associated with the mission of Celtic saints to England as well as with generations of later monks, only stones to be lashed by the sea winds; of Furness Abbey, where the Cistercians had flourished on a wild peninsula exposed to Scottish raids, or of Walsingham Priory ('England's Nazareth') deep in Norfolk, or of Hailes Abbey deep in Gloucestershire, which had displayed a phial of blood reputed to be Christ's, only some ruins; of Vale Royal Abbey in Cheshire, built magnificently in the intervals of castle construction for Edward I in Wales, nothing. When men saw that it was not going to be Oxford's cathedral, Oseney Abbey disappeared apart from one small building and the Great Tom bell (taken to Tom Quad in Christ Church). St Mary's Priory in Coventry was demolished once it was known that the diocese would have its cathedral in Lichfield. The Shakespeare quotation from Sonnet LXXIII cannot be resisted: 'Bare ruin'd choirs, where late the sweet birds sang'.

The Church of Scotland has done without bishops since 1690. However, bishops were kept on in the Church of England. They might be Protestant, and they might be humiliated by fellow-Protestants, but they were there and with them their cathedrals survived (with the exception of Peel Cathedral on the Isle of Man, disused after 1750). In the reign of Charles I there was a revival of ecclesiastical art, seen (for example) in the lovely window of Jonah contemplating Nineveh, painted in blue and gold to adorn the cathedral in Oxford. When the Church of England was overthrown itself in the 1640s, the link between king, bishop and cathedral protected none of them. But all three were restored in 1660, and the rebuilding of St Paul's Cathedral (and 50 parish churches) after the great fire of London was proof that the restored alliance meant something practical. In other cathedrals, too, the decade after the triumphant return of Charles II saw expensive restoration – of the fabric and fittings, the music and the clergy. Durham and Lichfield are the chief examples because there the destruction had been worst.

What restoration did not achieve was any policy for making the cathedrals work as centres of spiritual life. They were places where the services of the Book of Common Prayer were repeated by clergy and choir, often slackly, and attended by not very large numbers of the gentry or the old. Some who loved music enjoyed their services and the first 'Three Choirs Festival', which since then has combined Gloucester, Hereford and Worcester every year, was held in 1724; but the repertoire was limited, Tudor music having virtually died, 19th century music being unborn, Bach being virtually unknown and Handel or Haydn generally being thought unsuitable for performance in churches. Some who appreciated architecture visited the cathedrals, sometimes encouraged by engravings in books such as Sir William Dugdale's *Monasticon Anglicanum* (in three volumes published in the dark days of 1655-73) or John Britton's *Cathedral Antiquities* (in six volumes, 1814-35); but during the three centuries between the pilgrimages and the railways, tourism was laborious. Gradually, however, an interest in 'Gothic' architecture arose along with the assumption that the Middle Ages could do with improvement. A manual for architects was *Gothic Architecture Improved by Rules and Proportions* by Batty Langley (1742). Although the chief architects who were reckoned to know about old churches, James Essex and

James Wyatt, did not know much they were able to impose their schemes on even more ignorant clergymen. Often the results were lamentable, as were some attempts to fill medieval windows with pictures which would have been better on canvas. The nave of Norwich Cathedral is almost spoiled by the huge west window of 1854.

Deans and canons were now mostly well paid out of the endowments left to the cathedrals, but their numbers seemed larger than their duties. In some cathedrals there were still as many as a dozen canons or prebendaries, often holding other ecclesiastical posts as well. When the Church of England was challenged to minister to the millions in the new industrial towns, the scandal of these clergy, reputed to be rich but idle, became intolerable. 'The organ droned sadly in its iron cage to a few musical amateurs', wrote Charles Kingsley. 'The scanty service rattled in the vast building like a dried kernel too small for its shell. The place breathed imbecility and unreality, and sleepy life in death, while the whole nineteenth century went roaring on its way outside'. A reforming Bishop of London (C. J. Blomfield) asked what St Paul's Cathedral did for the people and answered: nothing.

In 1840 Parliament passed an Act of radical reform. Many canonries were abolished (including some 360 'prebends' subsidizing non-residentiary canons) and the salaries of the remaining clergy were standardized, usually at a lower level. The estates which had been given as the endowments of the cathedrals were gradually transferred to the Ecclesiastical (later the Church) Commissioners, who were to refund a fixed annual sum. This sum proved totally inadequate. Almost 100 years were to pass before the Commissioners made a more satisfactory deal with the cathedrals, retaining their estates but supporting a dean and two canons and contributing to the general expenses.

That was the setting in which the Victorian renewal of the cathedrals was slowly accomplished. A Royal Commission reported in 1854 with plans for reform. Conscientious deans and canons were appointed and introduced new standards of discipline and devotion. The music was transformed. And although the cathedrals continued to have severe problems in financing their regular life, special appeals to the public for the restoration of their fabrics met with a generous response. Often when the 20th century tourist admires a medieval church, the stones which are the subject of admiration were put there, or were repaired, by the Victorians. There was a similar revival in continental Europe. The French architect Eugène Viollet le Duc was a great student and exponent of medieval church-building as a science rather than as an exercise in mysticism. With the logical clarity that had marked the French Gothic master masons themselves, he compiled a *Dictionnaire raisonné* in ten volumes (1858-68). The completion of the soaring churches which had been left unfinished in Germany at the end of the Middle Ages (such as Cologne Cathedral, begun in 1248 and completed in 1880) reached heights unrivalled elsewhere. But the story of the Gothic revival in Britain is well worth telling.

Much of the early work which attempted to continue or revive medieval traditions was of poor quality; the little chapel of 1813 which became the core of the Roman Catholic cathedral in Edinburgh was one example. Naturally the best architects did better work; thus Wren was successful in the extension of Christ Church, Oxford, as a college, and Hawksmoor rescued Beverley Minster and built new west towers for Westminster Abbey. But the hearts of the best architects were not in the Gothic world – as we can see from Wren's classicizing plans for Old St Paul's, and Hawksmoor's for Westminster. Hawksmoor's six great churches in London largely avoided the memories of Gothic still evident in the work of Wren.

An essential preliminary to the recapture of the medieval vigour was a better understanding of the development of the medieval styles. These had emerged out of the practical plans of the master masons but had never been authoritatively distinguished and named. Generally acceptable terms for the different periods were established in an article reprinted as a booklet in 1817. The author was Thomas Rickman, who had worked in insurance in Liverpool before taking to architecture. But apart from the lasting success of his term 'Early English' he failed to secure the replacement of 'Gothic' by 'English' (and later attempts to replace 'Gothic' by 'Pointed' also failed to catch on). And perhaps because his personal faith was Quaker – about as far from medieval religion as may be imagined – the neo-medieval churches which he designed were lifeless.

The life and passion came with the young men of the Cambridge Camden Society, whose journal *The Ecclesiologist* (monthly from 1841) ardently influenced the Church of England to give visual shape to the High Church doctrines being spread from Oxford by the Tractarians. Above all, the evangelist of the movement was an architect's son who, between the ages of 14 and 40 (when he died), was aflame with enthusiasm for Gothic or 'Pointed' church-building. He was Augustus Pugin and his writing in the 1840s, particularly his *True Principles of Pointed or Christian*

The choir screen at Lichfield designed by George Gilbert Scott. A comprehensive scheme for the restoration of the cathedral was launched in 1856 and completed in 1908.

Architecture and his *Apology for the Revival of Christian Architecture in England*, proclaimed the movement's gospel. A Roman Catholic convert, he was an idealist and his attitude to the Middle Ages matched the romanticism of Sir Walter Scott's novels. But he was also practical. He had made his mark by doing all the detailed drawings for Sir Charles Barry's Houses of Parliament and one of his points was that pitched roofs threw off rain and snow.

Among the many converts to Pugin's architectural creed was the young George Gilbert Scott, who had been designing grim workhouses for the poor but who now became immensely confident, knowledgeable and resourceful in building or restoring about 750 buildings which ranged from St Pancras station and the Albert Memorial in London to many churches. Compiling a list of cathedrals and great churches in Britain which he did *not* restore would be a simpler task than making a list of those which he did. In his day perhaps the most active and influential architect in British history, he was later criticized for restoring too much and too little, for using machines instead of handicrafts and for escaping from the age of the machine. No judgement, favourable or hostile, on his very wide range of work is fair if it forgets that he had to negotiate all the time with clergy and other patrons — and that the alternative to the Victorian stonework would often have been ruin. When Kenneth Clark wrote *The Gothic Revival*, an 'essay' which deservedly went into many editions during and after 1928, he considered that the reputation of one so 'insensitive' could

The Victorian organ and choir screen in Chester.

not be revived. But later scholars have been less dismissive of his achievement. His sons George and John Oldrid and his grandson Giles were also leading ecclesiastical architects, although the younger George's career was cut short by mental illness, a tragedy which also overtook Augustus Pugin.

A number of these architects, and principally Sir George Gilbert Scott himself, were involved in the Victorian restoration of **Chester Cathedral**, which may be taken as a specimen of their rescue of old churches up and down the country. An artist, Dennis Creffield, wrote in 1988 that Scott 'went everywhere leaving a trail of disaster' and in Chester, 'managed to make a genuine medieval cathedral look like a municipal waterworks pretending to be one'. But is that fair?

In many ways Chester has been fortunate. Started by the Romans as a garrison town *(castra)* on the river Dee between Wales and Wirral, it has prospered mightily in many centuries including our own. Its galleried timber-and-plaster houses and shops make it one of the most charming towns in Britain. Its great church, of Saxon foundation, was rebuilt as a Benedictine monastery in the 12th century and enlarged by later medieval builders. The monks seem to have been on good terms with the townspeople; one of them wrote the earliest of the Chester Mystery plays, homely

biblical dramas which are still performed. Its cloister, chapter house and large refectory survived the Reformation, when it was made a cathedral; and Chester's good fortune lasted during the Second World War. But the cathedral had one near-fatal disadvantage: it was built of soft red sandstone, and was crumbling ('like a mouldering sandstone cliff' wrote Gilbert Scott). So from the 1840s to the 1930s it had to be very extensively rebuilt, with a new skyline, new roofs, new flying buttresses, new windows, new vaulted wooden ceilings, a new organ and new furnishings. Even the glorious choir stalls of the 1390s needed the attention of Victorian carpenters. The south transept, which had been divided off to form a large parish church, was reunited with a cathedral which was given an east-west unity by the removal of the stone *pulpitum* to the north transept. Gilbert Scott designed a spire but there was no money for that. And then Frank Bennett breathed new life into this ancient-and-modern building during his long time as dean (1920-37), abolishing admission charges and welcoming neighbours and visitors with an imaginative zest which revealed his love for people and gave his contemporaries a new idea of what a cathedral could be.

New Anglican Cathedrals

The last thing that Chester Cathedral needed was any physical extension. In Wales the medieval churches available as Anglican cathedrals were small in comparison, but the likely congregations would not be immense, so that here also restoration rather than extension has been needed (except in St Woollos in Newport). Gilbert Scott successfully restored chancels in Bangor and Brecon, and almost everything in St Asaph. We have already observed how the ancient glories of St Davids and Llandaff have been restored.

To make new Anglican cathedrals in England two town churches of the 18th century were available, needing only small extensions. They have so much white-and-gold elegance in them that it is tempting to speculate what their architects would have done if given Wren's opportunity to build a cathedral. In **Birmingham** a local architect, Thomas Archer, planned a church which was influenced by his study of the Baroque churches of Rome although comparatively sober with wooden galleries and some 'box' pews under the white plasterwork. It was consecrated in 1715. The deep colour came in the 1880s when Edward Burne-Jones designed, and William Morris made, four gorgeous windows. Only minor improvements have been necessary to support this church's promotion to cathedral rank in 1905. In **Derby** a much better known architect, James Gibbs (a Roman Catholic), used one of the designs he had prepared for St Martin-in-the-Fields in London. In St Martin's a new steeple was demanded and so one was made to rise rather awkwardly above the classical portico which now confronts Trafalgar Square, but in Derby a fine tower built some 200 years before could be retained. The church was consecrated in 1727 and made a cathedral 200 years later. The east end was extended in 1965-72 by Sebastian Comper. It is admired through the equally beautiful iron screen wrought by a local man, Robert Bakewell, in the 1740s. That was the time when the Young Pretender made Derby the southernmost point of the last Jacobite rebellion.

Four medieval parish churches in the north of England needed new east ends if they were to make convincing cathedrals. In **Newcastle upon Tyne** (where the making of a library and vestry in the 1730s had turned much of the south side into a Georgian town house) a new chancel of neo-medieval splendour was created by a local architect, R. J. Johnson. In **Wakefield** (where the most striking feature apart from Yorkshire's tallest spire was a chancel screen of 1635) the same thing was done by F. L. Pearson. The other churches became cathedrals after 1882 and their extensions show the decline in architectural energy. **Bradford** (1914) inherited from the 15th century a nave and tower that were sturdy. In 1951-65 it received from Sir Edward Maufe a new east end that was pleasant. **Blackburn** (1927) had one of the earliest churches of the Gothic revival, with a good nave designed in the 1820s. Here the east end has been built in stages since 1938 in simplified Gothic, with an octagonal lantern which is a whisper of Ely.

Two churches in the south of England needed not new chancels but new naves and in each case an architect had the modesty and skill to build as no more than a prelude to the medieval east end. In **Bristol Cathedral** the Norman nave had been pulled down early in the 1500s in order to build anew, presumably in the Perpendicular style as in Canterbury or Winchester. But money had run out, and until 1868 only the bottom of the aisle walls indicated where a nave should be. Then G. E. Street began building, in the year when he was appointed architect of the Law Courts in London (to George Gilbert Scott's discomfiture). By now people were so conscious of the marvels of the 14th century east arm of the cathedral that Street felt it his duty to harmonize. So the nave is broad and light, the aisles are the same height as the centre and there are tiercerons in the vault. But a close inspection shows that the Victorian architect was wise enough to avoid imitating the more daring details in the legacy of his medieval predecessor. On Street's death J. L. Pearson (and then his son, Frank) showed equal tact in completing the twin west towers, restoring much of the rest of the fabric and fitting out the choir for dignified worship.

In **Southwark Cathedral** tact was needed, not in order to avoid competition with the work of an eccentric medieval genius as in Bristol, but in order to avoid spoiling a chancel which was London's oldest surviving example of the Early English style. In 1212 fire had destroyed almost all of the Norman church at the south end of London Bridge, but the mighty Bishops of Winchester, whose London house was nearby, had financed the construction of an elegant church for the Augustinian canons. The chancel and retrochoir (behind the main altar) remain, saved from decay by a local architect, George Gwilt, in 1822-33. Transepts also remain, remodelled in the later Middle Ages. But in the 19th century this district of London became the scene of crowded poverty familiar to the readers of Dickens. The nave collapsed and was replaced by a structure with only one merit: it was cheap. If this historic church where Shakespeare had worshipped was to become the centre needed by the Church now trying to serve South London's teeming population, a new nave had to be built. Somehow the money was raised and Sir Arthur Blomfield was appointed as the architect who would achieve an Early English grace in the 1890s. Benefactors gave the fittings necessary to make the rescued church a cathedral in 1905.

How fortunate Bristol and Southwark were can be seen in Portsmouth and Sheffield. Admittedly the challenges both to architects and to fund-raisers were greater there. In **Portsmouth** a small church was built in the 1180s to serve a port which was little but growing. It was dedicated to St Thomas of Canterbury, perhaps with pilgrims from France in mind. The chancel survives. So does the nave of the parish church, rebuilt some 500 years later with a west tower which, with its lantern, became a lantern to Nelson and many others who used the adjacent naval dockyard. All this was spared in the World Wars although the area around was devastated. When the Isle of Wight and southern Hampshire were made an Anglican diocese in 1927, this seemed the obvious church to become a cathedral. But the solution to the problem of building an adequate new nave worthily was not obvious. Sir Charles Nicholson had a go but the money ran out and later schemes were also frustrated. It is hoped that in the 1990s the cathedral will at last be completed, with Michael Drury as architect.

The architectural history of the parish

church in the city centre of **Sheffield** is even more complicated. The Perpendicular church received various additions in later centuries, the most notable being Nicholson's Chapel of the Holy Spirit, dedicated in 1948 and intended as the chancel of a nave which was to run north-south. But the building of that nave was never started. The most recent additions have made the cathedral (so designated in 1914) serviceable but not large.

Leicester had a larger ancient parish church, next to the timbered Guildhall, with Perpendicular replacing Norman. But it was grievously decayed and it would be largely true to say that Victorian work designed by a number of architects replaced Perpendicular. Most of the furnishings of the choir are by Nicholson, made to celebrate the elevation to cathedral status in 1927. In Essex **Chelmsford** had another big old church which seemed the natural choice as the cathedral in 1913. And this church, too, had fallen into decay since the Middle Ages. But here the Perpendicular tower has not needed reconstruction and most of the rebuilding of the nave took place in 1801-3. Here Nicholson's work included more than furnishings; he extended the east end in the 1920s. Many of the present furnishings bravely belong to the 1980s and arouse discussion about their appropriateness in a medieval church. Certainly they fit into the modernity of a heavily-populated diocese.

In Suffolk the extension of an old church has been much more ambitious. When the county was made into an Anglican diocese in 1914, the historic associations of **Bury St Edmunds**

defeated the claims of the larger town of Ipswich and a recently-restored Perpendicular church (of St James) was available next to the gatehouse which had survived from the great medieval monastery. A fine hammerbeam roof over the nave had been added by Gilbert Scott. Probably this church was designed by John Wastell, a native of Bury, and it is hoped that one day there will be a central tower here which will be worthy of comparison with Wastell's tower in Canterbury. Meanwhile the east end, begun in 1959, is to the credit of the architect, Stephen Dykes Bower. It is clean in its modernity but also very dignified, and the furniture is worthy of it. The vibrant colour which enriches the general impression of light and light stone comes partly from a thousand kneelers, all different in design, yet all products of the proud spirit of Suffolk.

It is understandable that these new Anglican dioceses in England had no wish to add the building of completely new cathedrals to their problems. But some dioceses have made that leap of faith. The Anglicans in Scotland had to do so, for the ancient churches were now in the hands of the (Presbyterian) Church of Scotland. This Scottish Episcopal Church at first relied on William Butterfield, the imaginative architect of All Saints, Margaret Street, in London – and on the generosity of the young Earl of Glasgow. Little cathedrals, full of atmosphere, arose in Perth in 1849-50 (completed later) and then in Millport on Great Cumbrae as 'the cathedral of the isles'. After these experiments the Anglicans turned to the inevitable Gilbert Scott and gave him his chance to create, rather than restore, churches which would bring back the piety of the Middle Ages.

He built such churches in Dundee and Glasgow but his masterpiece was St Mary's Cathedral in **Edinburgh.** Two sisters, Barbara and Mary Walker, gave the site and much of the money needed for a noble essay in the style of the 13th century, with three spires and a central tower – and with conscious echoes of ruined Jedburgh and Kelso. Rivalled in Scotland only by Glasgow Cathedral, set amid green lawns, this great church was consecrated in the year after Sir George's death in 1878 and his son John Oldrid Gilbert Scott added what remained to be done. In one of the moments of enthusiasm in his presentation of *British Cathedrals* (1980) Paul Johnson has written that here, amid the Georgian politeness of this part of Edinburgh, 'one has the feeling of an intercontinental rocket at the moment of take off'.

Truro Cathedral was the first to be built for Anglicans in England since St Paul's. It seems to be both longer and taller than it actually is. It may be thought dull because it is a building which looks mainly Early English but is in fact mainly late Victorian. But its architect, J. L. Pearson, said that he wanted 'what will bring people soonest to their knees' and the fellow-Victorians who enabled him to build shared the strength of his faith. Truro Cathedral was not built in easy circumstances. Anglicanism was scarcely flourishing in Cornwall; since 1070 the nearest bishop had been in Exeter and since the Reformation the clergy, often disheartened and not seldom very eccentric, had been eclipsed by Methodist and other 'nonconformist' preachers as the people's pastors. Nor was the Cornish economy flourishing; undercut by foreign competition, tin mines were closing. But the first Bishop of Truro, E. W. Benson, appointed in 1877, was an ex-headmaster and future archbishop. He came from a canonry in Lincoln utterly determined that a new cathedral in a 'pure' medieval style – not Decorated as in Exeter – should be the centre of a revival of Catholic-type churchmanship with Victorian energy.

The old parish church of Truro, St Mary's, was (like many others which Benson found in Cornwall) small and decayed, but an aisle could be incorporated in the new church. The proposal to use English stone throughout was vetoed by Cornishmen, but Cornwall's own granite was available as the main building material. So funds were raised and within 30 years a cathedral arose, the eastern half in the 1880s, the nave and central tower by 1903, and the west towers by 1910. When J. L. Pearson died, his son Frank carried on as architect. All that needed to be added in the less confident time after the two World Wars was a chapter house in a severely modern style, with a nearby shop. Into the church have come many memorials recording Cornwall's history, old and modern; for example, in the lancet windows above the splendid high altar John Wesley is depicted beside Benson and Queen Victoria. Here is the religious focus of a county which is a Duchy and almost a nation, now given by its cathedral an added richness of memory, romance and beauty.

Roman Catholic Cathedrals

Anglicans were surprised to find themselves building these neo-medieval cathedrals on new sites. But the experience had become familiar to the Roman Catholics, whose numbers in Britain were swollen during the 19th century by some conversions from Anglicanism (at one stage thought likely to be very numerous) and by a flood of immigrants from famine-stricken Ireland. Three of the churches designated as cathedrals when the Pope appointed bishops for England in 1850 had been built in anticipation of that great day by Augustus Pugin. He persevered with great courage in his dream of reviving the glorious Middle Ages although in fact his churches were to be crowded by the urban poor. Despite financial backing from the Earl of Shrewsbury he had to build quickly and cheaply in brick, as when St Chad's was rushed up in Birmingham (1839-41), or in cheap stone which soon became grimy with industrial dirt, as in Nottingham (1840-42). He had to abandon his vision of a great tower and spire in St George's, Southwark (also built in the 1840s). In the Second World War his cathedral in Southwark was destroyed by bombs and since then many of the ornate fittings which he thought essential to the atmosphere in his other churches have been abolished in a crusade for simplicity. But he began a vigorous neo-medieval tradition.

One of Pugin's sons, Edward, built cathedrals for Northampton, Shrewsbury, Belmont near Hereford (the cathedral for the whole of Wales between 1855 and 95) and Wrexham; another, Peter Paul, for Cardiff (which replaced Belmont in 1920) and for Motherwell in Strathclyde; and a disciple, Matthew Hadfield, for Sheffield and Salford. If brick had to be used – as in Middlesbrough and Portsmouth – there could still be good dimensions. Some-times stone could be afforded and used well, as in Lancaster (with a high spire) and Aberdeen in the 1850s and in Leeds more modestly half a century later. And when a Duke of Norfolk was willing to pay for work of the first class, such work was provided. In Arundel a high-reaching French-style church by J. A. Hansom matched the duke's neo-medieval castle; it became a cathedral in 1965. A large Early English church by the two sons of Sir George Gilbert Scott, built in 1882-1910, overlooked Norwich; it became a cathedral in 1976.

This neo-medieval tradition exhausted itself and it may be said to lie buried in the cathedral built for Paisley (Glasgow) in the 1930s. But perhaps because of a greater confidence about what Catholicism really is in modern times, Roman Catholics broke away from the neo-medieval tradition more quickly than did the Anglicans. They have, for example, been less anxious that priest and people should face east, or that the church should be cruciform. The practical needs of the site, or the need to enlarge the church to accommodate a great congregation around the altar, have seemed far more important. And their best-known cathedrals in England have entirely abandoned the Gothic revival. It is a striking fact that Roman Catholicism has so largely shaken off the spell of the Middle Ages and has even moved out of the emphasis of the 'Counter-Reformation' on the separation of the clergy from a merely supportive laity. The key idea is now the pilgrimage of the People of God.

11 MODERN CATHEDRALS

Cardinal Manning bought a site for a Roman Catholic cathedral in **Westminster** but was not really interested in building it. His concern for the poor who were the majority of his flock absorbed his own energy and alienated the rich whose gifts would be needed. But his successor, Cardinal Vaughan, arrived in London with the firm intention of providing a symbol and centre for the Roman Catholicism which had now securely established itself in the capital and the nation. At first he wanted Benedictine monks as the staff, but they took fright at his masterful ways. And at first he envisaged an Italianate church (not wanting anything that looked like Westminster Abbey), but the architect he appointed, James Bentley, persuaded him that the main style should be Byzantine. The four domes are the children of a marriage between the west European tradition of a long nave and the great dome of *Hagia Sophia* in Byzantium. The glittering mosaics in the great porch at the west end are descended from the mosaics in Ravenna, once the western capital of the Byzantine empire. And there are features directly derived from Italy: the use of brick striped with white Portland stone and of

marble on the internal walls, the tall bell tower, the pulpit, the *baldacchino* or canopy over the high altar. The effect combines majesty and mystery. Disappointed as Bentley would have been by the failure to complete his design owing to shortage of funds, the effect may be heightened by the fact that much of the surface of the internal walls remains bare brick. For this may suggest the mystery of the night, covering mercifully all the troubles of the many who use this church for private prayer, lighting with stars the splendid corporate worship. And around those who pray are Eric Gill's 14 Stations of the Cross, carved during the First World War.

There are no transepts; the church is not cruciform. But chapels are placed on both sides of the nave beneath a gallery, with larger chapels beside the 'apse', the rounded east end. Together with these chapels, the crypt is used for the tombs of the archbishops. Really one unit, 104 metres (342 feet) long, almost 48 metres (150 feet) broad, more than 30 metres (100 feet) from floor to dome (although without the support of steel girders), Westminster Cathedral is a magnificent declaration and shelter of Roman Catholic piety. It was opened up to Victoria Street by a piazza built in 1976 as a richly deserved tribute.

In comparison, the Anglican cathedral of **Guildford,** accepted as a project in 1928, dogged by uncertainties and delays, but designed by Sir Edward Maufe and built between 1936 and 1961, is calm, clean and cool – a swimming pool, not a cascade. Like Westminster Cathedral, it is an essay in space. It, too, is a mass of brick with some limestone. It might have been exciting, and it still could be; it results from a noble ambition on the part of one of the dioceses created in 1927, and it has a huge tower which is helped to be a landmark by Stag Hill from which its bricks were made. Internally the brick is faced with almost white limestone. But the colours which might have enlivened this great church are pastel, the fittings and windows are domestic, the works of art are not masterpieces. Above the high altar, beneath a small window, is a long piece of plain cloth. The affluent county of Surrey, where church life flourishes, should not rest content with such a failure to set the religious imagination aflame.

The main style of Westminster Roman Catholic Cathedral is Byzantine.

The new Anglican cathedral of **Coventry** is, in contrast, an impressive art gallery. Like Guildford Cathedral it was planned before the liturgical movement became dominant in the Church, gathering the congregation round the altar; building began in 1956. Its acoustics are not good. Although it has a number of chapels people do not find it easy to pray in them; they are too public. In other words it is not a complete success as a church. And its small spire (a *flèche*) looks silly. But it deserves the fame which blazed around it when it was consecrated in 1962, for it is brilliantly successful (and not excessively expensive) as a building in which modern works of art are exhibited and give a strong message to the general public about the movement from evil to good, through life's struggles to light's simplicity and victory. And surely that is something which is a job for a modern cathedral. Were not medieval cathedrals exhibitions for pilgrims? The instruction given to the architect 'not to conceive a building but to conceive an altar – and to create a building round it' was obeyed to this extent: here is an altar which is plain but we look at it in awe because of the majestic art above it.

Sir Basil Spence was inspired to rise to the climax of his career as an architect in Coventry, and the artists whom he commissioned were inspired to give their best, by the tragedy of the Second World War. The noble church of St Michael, a cathedral since 1918, was shattered apart from its Perpendicular tower and spire

during the air raid which blitzed much of the city in 1940. The ruins were kept as a war memorial. The new cathedral was largely paid for by the nation as compensation for war damage and was largely regarded as an affirmation of spiritual recovery. Benjamin Britten's *War Requiem* was first performed in Coventry. 'Father, forgive' is inscribed on the altar amid the ruins, and statues by Epstein of Christ being doomed ('Behold the man!') and of St Michael subduing the Devil proclaim the eternal dimensions of what is forgiven. An international centre of reconciliation, built by young Germans, is housed here.

As one enters Coventry Cathedral, large doors of glass cut with the figures of angels and saints by John Hutton deny that there is any division between church and city, united by suffering and recovery. To the left and right are slatted walls. They seem rough stone from these doors (although they are inscribed with apt texts from the Bible) but if one looks back from the high altar, they glow with colour from glass by a number of artists, moving from green through red and blue to gold. Above the altar hangs a tapestry 23 metres (75 feet) high by Graham Sutherland. It exalts the triumphantly risen Christ. On either side are chapels which dramatize moments in the disciples' hard pilgrimage to the eternal altar – baptism in a font made of rock from Bethlehem against a background of John Piper glass in strong colours; a chapel of stone and iron which speaks with power of Christ's agony in

Sir Edward Maufe's design for Guildford Cathedral.

The immense tapestry which Graham Sutherland designed for the new Coventry Cathedral in 1952 shows the risen Christ surrounded by the symbols of the four gospels.

Gethsemane; a chapel of Christ the Servant linked with industry; a chapel of Christian unity shaped like a crusader's tent. All this is held together by red sandstone and concrete, although the design is sufficiently Gothic to have aisles and a vault-like roof and the church-builders of the late Middle Ages would have understood why the structure is a framework for coloured glass. But everything is also held together by a post-war vision, unforgettably linked by Graham Sutherland's art with the everlasting gospel of the Bible.

It is inevitable that we should end this brief history of British cathedral-building in **Liverpool,** for two fascinating modern cathedrals rise in that proud but tragic city above the Mersey and when taken together they pose – as dramatically as could be imagined – questions about the future.

Liverpool has never been a city of widely spread wealth. Up until 1600 it was a village with about 500 inhabitants. Then it became a great port for the Atlantic trade, but the destitution of many of those who sailed from this port – the slaves captured in Africa, the families fleeing from hunger to North America or Australia – was almost matched by the poverty of most of those who worked in the docks or factories, including hundreds of thousands who came from Ireland, Wales or Scotland with very few strengths, apart from a sectarian religion, Catholic or Protestant. This fighting faith amid bitter suffering helps to explain why both Liverpool's cathedrals were conceived on a grandiose scale. They were the affirmations of a city – or rather of its two distinct communities, Catholic and Protestant – that faith had made the suffering endurable. The pennies of the poor were given. But another explanation is also valid. The prosperous trade of the port, almost all of it from or to the empire, produced during the first half of the 20th century a feeling which was still militant and still hardworking but much more confident. And the trade had made a considerable number of men very rich. Liverpool now possessed the most splendid civic buildings in Britain. Why should it not have spectacular cathedrals?

In 1901 Bishop F. J. Chavasse led a group which decided that 21 years had been long enough for a new Anglican diocese to be without a cathedral and chose an architect aged 22, Giles Gilbert Scott. Selected from among more than 100 competitors, he promised to build the largest Anglican church in the world, Gothic but modern, with a massiveness matching and exceeding any Norman work and with twin towers matching and exceeding any Perpendicular dream. Bishop Chavasse was delighted. And almost 30 years later Archbishop Downey decided that

Liverpool Cathedral embodies the vision of Sir Giles Gilbert Scott.

the Roman Catholic Church must compete. He purchased a site, formerly a vast workhouse for Liverpool's poor, not far from what he regarded as the cathedral of the heretics, and employed the leading architect of the day, Sir Edwin Lutyens, to build here a domed Baroque cathedral. It would be exceeded in the Roman Catholic world only by St Peter's, Rome. In the 1850s Edward Pugin had designed a cathedral on another site, almost as grand but in his father's neo-medieval style. The Lady chapel alone had been built and had sufficed as a church for the parish in Everton. Lutyens scorned that plan as lacking in ambition. He admired Wren's plan for St Paul's before it was made cruciform but thought that it, too, was on the small side.

In the end neither Scott nor Lutyens achieved his initial intention. The foundation stone of the Anglican cathedral was laid in 1904 but the first part to be built, the Lady chapel, owed more to the veteran architect G. F. Bodley who had been appointed to collaborate with this youngster. When Bodley died Scott drastically revised the plan. The rest of his cathedral was to be much simpler: for example, it was to have only one tower, 100 metres (331 feet) high. Most of its red sandstone (quarried in nearby Woolton) was to be plain, but near the top was to be decoration inspired by great Gothic churches in Spain and in Albi, deep in the south of France. The style was to be a combination of his own love of plain massiveness (which in London created the Battersea and Bankside power-stations and Waterloo Bridge, and in Cambridge the equally monumental University Library) and his grandfather's love of the decoration of the 14th century. Choir and nave were both to have three bays only and the impact was to be derived from the sheer size of the arches, the largest ever to be built in a Gothic manner. There were to be vast coloured windows, mainly by James Hogan, but they were not to distract from the sense of space (and in fact only the rich west window by Carl Edwards, completed after Scott's death in 1960, is a rival to the stone). There was to be sculpture (mostly by Carter Preston); there was to be a chapter house (the gift of Freemasons); there were to be chapels – but these also were to be subordinated to the creation of staggering spaces. And even this revised plan was never fully translated into stone. Building continued despite the two World Wars, despite the inter-war depression and despite the post-war decline of the empire and of imperial trade; and sufficiently rich benefactors were found to pay for each phase of the slow project. But it became obvious that the plan for the west end must be modified if the completion of a cathedral consecrated and used since 1924 was to be celebrated in 1978. It was.

Since then, other changes in the interests of practicality have been made; for example, one of the great porches has been turned into a restaurant. In 1988 it was announced that a residential college with conference facilities was to be built next to the cathedral. What cannot be changed is a certain lack of practicality when it comes to worship. Here is a basic problem in architectural vision which is not entirely solved by the imagination with which many services have been planned. For the high altar, although prominent, is distant from the congregation and the nave, although it makes a superb hall for concerts or drama, is lower than the central space and separated from it by a bridge. This bridge may be a 'stroke of genius' as Paul Johnson has claimed, but is in curious contrast with the general tendency in modern times to unify a church by uniting a congregation round an altar. A confusion is revealed, for the Anglicans who were Scott's patrons mostly desired a Protestant emphasis, while he was Roman Catholic. There seems to have been some uncertainty about whether altars are needed.

Sir Edwin Lutyens saw the foundation stone of his vast Roman Catholic cathedral laid amid great solemnities in 1939 and his crypt was built very finely. But his full dream was never realized. The Second World War halted work and after that it was obvious that the necessary millions could never be found to pay for the colossus which was intended to surmount the crypt. In 1958 Archbishop (later Cardinal) Heenan opened the crypt for use – which since then has not been very extensive – and the next year he bravely announced that a new architect was being sought to build a cathedral above ground level for only £1 million. The decision to withdraw from the extravagance of competition with the Anglicans was one of the early signs of a new spirit in interchurch relations – a spirit which since then has flourished.

Sir Frederick Gibberd, an Anglican who had designed London Airport, was entrusted with this job (the modern word seems right). He used the Lutyens crypt as a platform, making a piazza for Mass on great occasions if the weather permits, and on the same level he built a circular cathedral in concrete with a modest dome. As in Coventry there is good stained glass, by John Piper and Patrick Reyntiens, and there are some works of art. But this is no art gallery. Moreover, here the impression left is not at all like that conveyed by the Anglican cathedral. Here is no creation by the wealth of the few; low-budget as it is, this church has still needed loans which will have to be repaid. Here is no insistence on the luxury of perfection; this church soon needed expensive roof repairs which were a reminder of the dangers of false economy. Here is no memory of the Middle Ages; the exterior is bleakly and brutally, the interior more mildly, of the 1960s. And here is no empty space; Gibberd's patrons knew exactly what they wanted in the light of the Second Vatican Council and everything is subordinated to the central altar in white marble. More than any other great church in Britain, this cathedral shows what the 'liturgical' movement means. Construction took only five years, 1962-67.

In the circumstances it is surely no discredit to the Roman Catholics that they never built the sublime cathedral which Lutyens imagined. Nor is it to the discredit of the Anglicans that they *did* build so expensively, for their plan was made long before unemployment dominated the real life of Liverpool. They had already been building for forty years when the war ended and it would have been a gesture of despair had a cathedral which was so prominent been left half-built. But probably many who have visited the two cathedrals at the two ends of Hope Street have felt that neither gives a complete reply to the question of how to build a great cathedral in a style which does not hark back to a vanished world.

The circular nave of Liverpool's Roman Catholic Cathedral.

Scott's cathedral may be said to give half of the answer. It teaches that, to be worthy and enduring, the vision and the craftsmanship must be generous and excellent. Gibberd's cathedral adds that a church must be built with a clear purpose; worship by clergy and people around an altar. The same lesson is taught more excellently by the small and simple cathedral which Scott built in granite for Roman Catholics in Oban on the west coast of Scotland in the 1930s and 40s, and by the small Roman Catholic cathedrals built in concrete in Clifton (Bristol) in the 1970s and in Coulby Newham near Middlesbrough in the 1980s. But those admirable churches cannot be called great. The question about a great church remains. Expounding his dream for Liverpool, Bishop Chavasse said: 'it must be a cathedral of the people, built by them, thronged by them, loved by them; their pride, their glory, their spiritual home'. It can be argued that in Britain a really great cathedral of that character, in a modern or post-modern style, remains to be built.

BRITAIN'S
LIVING CATHEDRALS

12 CANTERBURY

Canterbury Cathedral.

When the determination of Pope Gregory the Great turned a highly nervous group of monks in Rome into a team of slightly less nervous missionaries, his plan for the English Church was clear – and also logical, in theory. It was based on what was remembered of the time when Rome had included Britain in its political empire. In the province of York twelve bishops were to be led by an archbishop and there was to be a province of London, identical in structure and equal in status. But things did not work out like that. Anglo-Saxon England proved difficult to convert and before industrialization the north was sparsely inhabited. The only secure base for the Christian mission in its early years was Kent – a small but influential kingdom close to Christian France. Kent already had a French Christian princess as queen before any missionary arrived. Even when the north was converted and persuaded to adopt Catholic (not Celtic) customs, the province of York was never prosperous enough to sustain the claim to equality which was made periodically by its archbishops, amid much vexation and scandal, right up to 1353. And so the senior bishop or 'Primate of All England' has always taken his title from a country town in Kent, although his widely-ranging work, national and international, has meant that he could not spend much of his time in Canterbury.

The Archbishops of Canterbury were the leaders of English church life, sometimes saints and often the chief counsellors of kings, for almost 600 years before a building arose which we should recognize as Canterbury Cathedral. The first archbishop, St Augustine, dedicated the first cathedral to Christ about five years after baptizing Ethelbert, King of Kent, in 597. There had been a modest royal palace nearby, now given to the archbishop, and a Roman mosaic floor has been excavated. That cathedral was enlarged in the 8th century. After a convenient fire a still larger one was built by the Normans – massive, plain and, it seems, almost exactly the duplicate of the monastic church of St Etienne in Caen, where Archbishop Lanfranc had been abbot before being brought to England as William the Conqueror's most trusted agent. The dimensions of the nave were the same as those of Canterbury's present nave. The north-west tower survived until

These great Norman arches in the north choir aisle were built about 1180.

1834, when it was demolished in order to make room for a duplicate of the south-west tower built in the 15th century. But only a few fragments of Lanfranc's cathedral are now visible.

The east end of that great church was pulled down in the time of Lanfranc's successor as archbishop, St Anselm, in order to make room for a more spacious and sophisticated choir. The crypt, which survives, was begun in 1096. It is high and light enough for people to be able to see the vigorously imaginative carvings on the capitals of the pillars, which constitute the finest collection of Norman sculpture in England. Probably they were copied from pattern books and carved on the spot. Often the subject of this sculpture is animals fighting, not inappropriate in a Norman colony whose crude brutality caused much distress to the saintly and scholarly Anselm. But sometimes these beasts make music: in the chapel of St Gabriel, beneath a great wall-painting of Christ, a goat sitting on a dragon plays a recorder while the dragon bites his arm, another recorder is played by a fox, a winged creature plays a violin and a griffin plays a harp. Two impressive ornamented towers and two east transepts complete with chapels also remain

from the Norman era. Some wall-paintings have survived to suggest why this Norman choir was called 'glorious'. But fire wrecked it in 1174, only 40 years after its completion. A contemporary, Gervase, has left a vivid description of the calamity and the laments.

That fire of 1174 was, however, the real beginning of Canterbury Cathedral as we know it, since the monks put a French master mason, William of Sens, in charge of the reconstruction and he persuaded them to build anew in stone and in a style imported from France. The stone came from Caen, the style from the new cathedral in his home town. Compared with the Norman style to which England had grown accustomed the piers are slighter, taller and closer to each other; they culminate in 'capitals' (carved tops) which are more elaborate, being Corinthian in character; and the arches are more pointed. The storey above, with twin arches in each bay, is much less emphasized. The broad vault is in stone, with each bay divided into six parts. All that is an adaptation of what can still be seen in Sens. But some enrichments to the French design were added in Canterbury. The most striking is the use of Purbeck 'marble' in detached shafts. This was an innovation which was to be widely copied in England.

Some conservative touches, also departing from the Sens plan, may have consoled those who still mourned the fire of 1174. The piers in the arcade were alternatively circular and octagonal, as in the Norman work. The main arches in the triforium were still round and there was still a gallery in the clerestory. Most of the walls of the aisles were conserved in order to retain Norman chapels which had survived, giving the east end of the cathedral the shape of a wasp. But the quality of the new carving caused Gervase to comment that it looked as if a chisel had been used instead of an axe. Some experts think that there were no new tools, but what was essentially different was that the walls of a church had been imagined as graceful works of art.

Architecture in England took another decisive step forward when William of Sens, incapacitated by a fall from scaffolding, handed over to William the Englishman as master mason. This second William was as innovative as the Frenchman. He raised the easternmost part of the cathedral by 16 steps above a new crypt. Here the Trinity Chapel led into the final chapel or *corona* (from the Latin for 'crown'). The piers cunningly maintain the same height as those in the choir but are all round and all in Purbeck 'marble'. Viewed from outside the *corona* is a puzzle, for the medieval builders never completed it and their intentions are unknown. But we clearly see another architectural revolution: the walls, projecting beyond the Norman work, could frame a dozen large windows and still be supported by flying buttresses outside. There was no precedent for this in England and even in France the device was not many years old. It was vital to the new French ideal of a great church as a tall cage of stone filled with radiant glass. Less than half the medieval glass remains here and what has survived has been much restored. But it is worthy of comparison with the windows of Chartres Cathedral — where 2045 square metres (22,000 square feet) of medieval glass survives — which is not surprising, for the glass was probably made in Chartres. The action in these windows is as full of vigour as in a modern strip-cartoon although the costumes are of about 1220. There are important older windows in Canterbury Cathedral with biblical subjects as tradition dictated, but these 'miracle' windows in the corona are Britain's oldest large collection of stained glass.

Their subject is the celebration of the miracles already' achieved by St Thomas of Canterbury. Archbishop Thomas Becket had been murdered by four knights coming from the court of Henry II, in the north-west transept one December evening in 1170. He had been inspired during his unedifying quarrel with the King (over the unglamorous subject of the legal privileges of the clergy) by memories of Canterbury's Anglo-Saxon saints. Made a saint in 1173, he triumphed in his tomb, becoming a magnet to pilgrims, including the penitent Henry II. Now the symbol of the Church against the State, of the people against the King, his fame spread throughout Europe. Of the very many representations of his life, death and miracles, many have perished but one that is special survives in the lovely glass of St Lucy's chapel in Oxford's cathedral, made about 1340. Through three and a half centuries the pilgrims came: some men with wealth, some story-tellers as in Chaucer's *Canterbury Tales* (the first large-scale masterpiece in the English language), and many more common, inarticulate folk glad of the chance of a holiday. Some 50 years after the martyrdom King Henry III, Archbishop Stephen Langton (who was responsible more than anyone else for Magna Carta) and the monks moved the saint's body from the crypt to a shrine in the finished Trinity Chapel. The shrine was covered by gold and jewels: no tomb in the world was more splendid. Only the lovely worn marble pavement which had surrounded it was left after Henry VIII had taken vengeance on Becket's defiance of the monarchy — but as one climbs from the nave into the choir, and from the presbytery into the Trinity Chapel, one understands why the pilgrims were dazzled. It may be significant that Chaucer never felt able to describe the end of the pilgrimage.

St Thomas Becket: a window made for Canterbury about 1220.

If a monastery is meant to be a place where men are turned into humble saints, Christ Church, Canterbury, does not appear to have been much of a monastery. Its monks were often in dispute with the archbishops, with the townspeople and above all with the rival Benedictine monastery a few yards away, St Augustine's. But while proud wealth and the pressures of tourism made holiness difficult, Christ Church did achieve beauty. The tombs which it raised for that ruthless general, the Black Prince, and for that conscience-tormented King, Henry IV, are beautiful. Its monastic buildings still adorn the spacious precincts, either in grand ruin or in use by the clergy or the boys and girls of the King's School.

A Norman staircase led up to a hall for the reception of one class of pilgrim; a wooden 'pentise' or covered walk of 1390 sheltered the more privileged on their way to better lodgings in the Cellarer's Hall; and the house which was a hotel for princes is still called after Meister Omer, the monastery's official for whom it was built in the 13th century. A water tower was the centre of a system of pipes which kept monks, servants and guests remarkably healthy even before the time of Thomas Becket. The large and lofty chapter house where the monks met daily survives. A superb barrel vault of Irish oak has covered it since the early 1400s, when the cloister was largely reconstructed with more than 800 heraldic shields in its vaults. The Christ Church Gateway was rebuilt ornately in 1517 by men who did not know that the monastery was to be dissolved some 20 years later.

The resources of the archbishop and the monks – who could co-operate at times – were used with supreme effect to dignify the last few hundred yards of the way taken by pilgrims as, having come on horse, mule or foot from London, Dover, Southampton or wherever, they began the ascent to the shrine. Before he was murdered by a mob during the Peasants' Revolt of 1381 Archbishop Simon Sudbury had paid for the demolition of most of Lanfranc's nave. Ten years later Thomas Chillenden was elected prior. He collaborated with Henry Yevele, the leading architect of the day, and to their vision we owe the present nave and west transepts. In his nave in Westminster Abbey, Yevele had been instructed to change little in the plan approved by Henry III for the choir; in Westminster Hall he had been told to keep much of the Norman work, but now no limitation was placed on his genius. Even the transept where Becket had been martyred could be modernized – although that was left to the last and the old floor level was preserved. In the nave, as in the choir, the arches of the arcade are high. Light streams in through the tall windows of the aisles and to a lesser extent through the clerestory, beneath which the triforium has been reduced to mere panelling. The vertical shafts are continuous, so that the eye is not interrupted in its delighted journey up to the lierne vault. This forest of stone was finished by 1405. It led to a massive stone *pulpitum* in which were placed statues of six kings from Edward the Confessor to Henry VI. Later a window showing the family of Edward IV was placed above the site of 'the Martyrdom'. The point was made: the monks and the pilgrims were under royal patronage.

The old central tower, called the Angel Steeple because of its crowning decoration, had been demolished by 1430, but its replacement had to wait for another 60 years. The 'Bell Harry' tower was mostly paid for by Cardinal Morton, celebrating peace under the first of the Tudor Kings, Henry VII. The architect was John Wastell, who achieved another masterpiece in the vaulting of King's College Chapel in Cambridge. By using almost half a million bricks concealed by stone he was able to persuade the cardinal that the tower would be light enough to stand if its height were raised to 71.5 metres (235 feet) above the ground during its construction. Even so, large stone girders had to be added to strengthen the piers which took the weight in the nave below. 'Bell Harry' has stood and it is remembered for its dominating height, but it is also a tower which can give pleasure if one has the patience to admire its details. Here the vigour of wall arcading has developed from geometry into poetry. Inside the cathedral the fan vault of this tower, above the steps into the choir, is very beautiful.

The centuries after the dissolution of the monastery have added to the monuments in a cathedral which has continued to epitomize English church history – although between the execution of Charles I and the death of Queen Victoria Canterbury saw much less of its archbishops, whose medieval palace was burned down by a Puritan mob. The biggest changes could never have been expected in the Middle Ages. The almost world-wide expansion of the Anglican Communion amid the colonialism of the 19th century has been followed by the expansion of tourism, much of it international. When the medieval pilgrimages ceased Canterbury became a quiet country town. It is so no longer. Visitors crowd the streets which were extensively rebuilt after the bombing of the 1940s. They come from many nations.

When the word 'Anglican' ceased to refer to members of the Church of England only, and when the Anglican Communion turned out to be a loosely-organized fellowship both wider and more enduring than the British empire, the question had to be asked: what makes an

The choir at Canterbury, looking towards the Trinity Chapel where the Shrine of St Thomas once stood.

Anglican? The simplest answer is that an Anglican is a member of a church which is in communion with the Archbishop of Canterbury, sending its bishops to consult with him once every ten years in the Lambeth Conference and honouring his office as the focus of a unity which tries to combine Catholic, Protestant and liberal elements. So nowadays Canterbury Cathedral makes much of 'St Augustine's chair' (which is probably Stephen Langton's chair, made in the 13th century). It has become in a sense the mother church of more than 50 million Anglicans.

Modern pilgrims, whether or not they are Anglicans, are welcomed by many efforts to make the cathedral's past live in ways which will make sense to them. Becket's murder continues to fascinate. It was interpreted by T. S. Eliot's play *Murder in the Cathedral*, first performed in the chapter house in 1935, and by several modern biographies and novels. A chapel of 'saints and martyrs of our own time' in the *corona* was made in the 1980s, as was a dramatic altar of painful sacrifice at the scene of the murder. And part of the fascination is that here was a martyr with obvious human faults. To our time he says that in the glorious Church of Christ humanity is needed.

13 CHICHESTER

Is it the most typically but quietly English of all the country's great churches? The scene is English as the spire of Chichester Cathedral arises between the sea and the Downs, above a delightful town. And this church is a comfortable English home for many beautiful things, ancient and modern; the modern works of art fit in precisely because the architecture in their background is unobtrusive. It is a home for people who lead unflappable lives; the monument to the first person killed by a train — Walter Huskisson, Chichester's MP, killed in 1839 — clothes him in Roman dress. Sir Nikolaus Pevsner put it like this: 'in its even temperament it was the perfect Anglican cathedral long before there was a Church of England'.

Chichester was made the seat of the bishop of the South Saxons in 1075. Previously the bishops had been based in Selsey, on the coast. Bishop Ralph de Luffa built a cathedral in the 1090s and 1100s, using stone from the Isle of Wight. As can still be seen in the nave, the transepts and the choir below the clerestory, the architecture was plain, without aisles and with the gallery almost as high as the arcade of arches. But when a fire caused much damage in 1187 a new set of masons, probably including men who had worked on the choir of Canterbury, modernized the cathedral by adding shafts of Purbeck 'marble' as decoration and by building stone vaults for the sake of safety.

A square-ended retrochoir now replaced the Norman apse, and its combination of a Norman arcade of arches with an Early English triforium (the opposite combination to Canterbury's) is a successful example of the Transitional style. In 1279 this retrochoir received the shrine of a sainted bishop who had once been a poor student in Oxford sharing a coat with another. While a bishop he walked through Sussex on foot, sustained by a vegetarian diet and a faith expressed in his famous prayer that he might see Jesus more clearly, love him more dearly and follow him more nearly day by day. What a contrast there is between St Richard of Chichester and Canterbury's proud Thomas Becket!

Some later medieval additions lacked the dignity and grace of the retrochoir. This is unfortunately true of the long and narrow Lady chapel (in the Decorated style), of the huge windows in the transepts and of the bell tower built in the 15th century outside the nave — although the tower has an interest as being the only survivor of its class in English cathedrals. A lack of grace is, however, not true of the Arundel screen, restored to its position between the nave and the choir in 1961, some 500 years after its construction. No criticism can be made of the misericords under the choir stalls, or of the charming cloister, three-sided, vaulted in wood about 1400 and originally surrounding a 'Paradise' or graveyard. And one realizes how busily devout the medieval cathedral was when one begins to count up the number of chapels — some of them in the nave, where double aisles were added in the 13th century.

Thoughts about medieval religion are challenged to go deeper than usual in Chichester's south choir aisle. There one finds a magnificent tomb. In an effigy which seems to be lifelike (a departure from the earlier medieval practice), it commemorates Bishop Robert Sherburne, who died, over 90 years old, in 1536 just as the storms of the Reformation were beginning to destroy the England where he had cut a splendid, energetic and astute figure. Not far away are paintings which he commissioned to show the long lines of Bishops of Chichester and Kings of England,

The retrochoir of Chichester combined a Norman arcade of arches with an Early English triforium in the 1190s. The tapestry by Ursula Benker-Schirmer (1985) is above the site of the shrine of St Richard, Bishop of Chichester (1245-1253).

with Church and State in close alliance. The kings included Henry VIII – in vain. But on either side of this monument to fallen power and pomp is a pair of stone panels sculptured in the second half of the 12th century. The art is profoundly but unsentimentally devout. In one, Jesus enters the house of Martha and Mary. In the other, he raises their brother Lazarus from the dead. The faces around him express grief, wonder and indifference. His own face changes: first he seems to be gathering up the power of the spirit, then to be relaxing in triumphant love. St Richard must have seen these panels, which probably belonged to the *pulpitum*, dismantled in order to make way for the Arundel screen. It is probable that Chichester once possessed a whole series of such sculptures – painted, with precious stones in the eye sockets. These two were treated as rubble before being rescued in 1829. A fragment of a third is preserved in the library.

Tempests of Protestant bigotry destroyed much that was beautiful, including almost all the medieval glass; a familiar tale. In Chichester unusually fierce storms also blew in from the sea. In 1210 the south-west tower fell down; in 1635 the north-west tower; in 1861 the central tower and spire. But they were all rebuilt, the north-west tower as recently as 1901, matching its restored medieval twin, and the central tower and spire as a replica of the work of about 1400 by Sir George Gilbert Scott in the 1860s.

In the 1960s and later new beauty has been added, thanks largely to the initiatives of Dean Walter Hussey. A font by John Skelton and a pulpit by Geoffrey Clarke are clearly of our time. So are two tapestries on either side of the screen erected by Bishop Sherburne over the high altar. One is by John Piper; the other, made by Ursula Benker Schirmer in 1985, is a symbol of Anglo-German reconciliation. In these tapestries all the colour of a vibrant modernity explodes, as it does in paintings by Graham Sutherland and Patrick Procktor. The modern windows include one by Marc Chagall, mainly in flaming red. It is an interpretation of the praise of God by all creation in the last of the Hebrew psalms.

14 DURHAM

The view from the 18th-century Prebends' Bridge is famous. Above the river Wear and its wooded cliffs you see the massive cathedral with the bishop's castle not far from it. And at first sight Sir Walter Scott's line, which is carved on the balustrade of the bridge, seems exactly right: 'Half church of God, half castle 'gainst the Scot'. It is also right that the line is ambiguous. Does it refer to the scene as a whole, or is the cathedral itself half a castle? For in the Middle Ages the Bishops of Durham were virtually viceroys in this border country, with their own courts and coinage. Since the diocese extended to the border with Scotland until 1881, they were expected to organize military resistance to invaders from the north, who were still causing trouble in the reign of Elizabeth I. Much of their privilege and wealth lingered on into the 1830s. And their cathedral was appropriately strong and rich — so rich, even after the Reformation, that when reform was in the air in the 1830s the Dean and Chapter were able to found a university out of their revenues combined with some of the bishop's wealth, so that students moved into the bishop's castle. But if one asks why bishops who were in the thick of the politics of England under Norman rule had the will to build such an enormous church, and had the right to be at least the equal of any lay baron in the north, and owned this mighty castle among others, the historian's answer is clear. Cathedral and castle were built chiefly in order to impress the people who would observe them day by day: England's natives.

An Anglo-Saxon cathedral was built here because of Cuthbert, a humble saint. A shepherd boy on the hills outside Edinburgh, a monk in the Celtic Church, a bishop who accepted the new form of Catholicism based on Rome, he united many traditions in the Christian life of the north in his own life, which was one of uncanny holiness and self-denial. After some missionary work in Northumbria from a base on the 'Holy Island' of Lindisfarne, he became a hermit on the smaller Farne Island, then as now the home of seals, then as now battered by the North Sea. His body seems to have been so emaciated that it was mummified by the salt sand in which it was buried in 685 – 'uncorrupt' to the devout amazement of many generations. After various journeys it was brought in 995 to this rocky height where the Wear looped, so that it and the clergy who brought it could be secure from the raiding Vikings. A stone church with two towers, each topped by a brass pinnacle, was built as a shrine. The body of St Cuthbert is still in Durham Cathedral, although when it was last seen there was no flesh on the bones.

William the Conqueror had trouble from rebels as well as invaders. His main response to the North was to devastate it, but when the last Anglo-Saxon bishop had been starved to death in prison a Norman was appointed in his place and was encouraged to found a Benedictine monastery at the mouth of the Wear – which he did before being killed in a riot. His successor was a Norman monk, William, who came from the French town of St Carileff, also called St Calais. He stood no nonsense. He brought the monks up the river to Durham; he purchased the rights of the Earl of Northumberland, so that he increased his control over the country-side as well as over the monks; and with masons whose names have disappeared he pulled down the Anglo-Saxon church and (from 1093) built about a third of the cathedral which we see.

Durham Cathedral rises above the River Wear.

The site of St Cuthbert's shrine in Durham.

The architecture may have been influenced by observations made during the three years when the bishop had been in exile in France, accused of treason against King William Rufus. The architect himself may have been recruited from France as a result of a contact in that period. An unusually tough local sandstone was used. The cathedral was completed under William's successor, Rannulf Flambard, who was the unquestionably loyal servant of William Rufus as chaplain and prime minister because he was himself a thorough rogue. The two west towers were raised in different periods – half by the Normans and half during the 13th century. The contrast between the plain Norman base and the later arcading is instructive.

What is astonishing about the cathedral is not only its size but also the pioneering courage, speed and skill of its architecture. In the nave the message is unmistakably a show of masculine strength. The windows are larger than in the Norman work of the previous century. In the arcade the arches are much taller than the gallery and the eye cannot hurry as it moves along the enormous pillars. These are separated by plainer piers which are almost like walls, and are deeply incised with grooves in one or other of three geometrical patterns. The grooves were originally painted or perhaps filled with metal. There are no earlier examples of grooves on this scale in England (although this feature was to be copied in Waltham Abbey in Essex, where the manor belonged to the Bishops of Durham, at Dunfermline in Scotland and elsewhere). And even without this decoration we know that these pillars are meant to impress; they are far larger than is needed for structural purposes. Another form of carved decoration is found on the walls of the aisles, where the interlocking arches are one of the things which the Normans learned from their contacts with Islam. We therefore have far less sense than in Ely (for example) of the nave being an unadorned prelude to the choir.

There is also less of the anticlimax which may be felt when, as in Ely or Peterborough, the strong walls are seen to support a mere wooden roof, for in Durham the nave received ribbed vaults in stone in the mid-1130s. The only ribbed vaults in England earlier than these were also achieved in this cathedral, in the choir and its aisles, but the difficulty of what had been done about 1104 is indicated by the fact that the choir vaults had to be rebuilt in the next century. And the nave of Durham has another pioneering feature: four of its vaults are separated by great transverse arches which are pointed. They are there for a practical purpose but the Norman style is in transition to the pointedness of Early English. Between the great pillars thin shafts of stone run up from the floor to these arches. Architecture is beginning to be vertical in emphasis – to be in Hugh Braun's phrase 'the architecture of transcendency'.

Today the cathedral may seem empty and colourless, which may contribute to the image of merciless power. But the church which the Normans left behind was for 400 years the centre of a great monastery, and its appearance must have been very different. Whitewashed externally and richly decorated internally, lit by coloured glass almost all of which has been destroyed, it was full of treasures of gold, silver and fabric. When under Elizabeth I an anonymous veteran wrote nostalgically about the monastic days from personal memories, it was not the architecture that was chiefly in his mind and heart. It was the memory of the solid assurance of the life and worship of the monks, who were surrounded by much evidence of their consecrated wealth. A relic of this tradition is the splendid knocker made in the 12th century for the north door. A fugitive from justice using it was assured of temporary sanctuary in the church although eventually he would have to flee the country. The monks' chapter house, cloister, refectory, kitchen, dormitory and prison survive. They are all on a large scale, as are the houses which were occupied by the dean and canons when the monks had gone.

Medieval bishops and monks joined forces to add to their architectural heritage out of a part of their ample revenues. Some great stone window frames have survived the loss of their glass – although the most prominent window, the rose at the east end, is a copy made in the 18th century of the original 15th-century window. The 'Galilee' chapel at the west end was begun in 1189 on the orders of the first of the really magnificent Bishops of Durham, Hugh de Puiset. The intention had been to build a Lady chapel in the normal place, at the east end. But there the rocky ground slopes downward and the site proved too difficult. So the Lady chapel of Durham Cathedral was put (uniquely) at the west end although that meant

An angel, one of the many small carvings on the Neville screen, which dates from about 1380.

The nave of Durham, the climax of Norman architecture in England, was begun in 1093. The stone vaulting was revolutionary.

ending the entrance to the nave through the great west portal. The new chapel was large and light. Originally it was a mass of colour on walls and in windows. It was at the disposal of the bishop for ceremonial or business purposes and the monks used it for the finale of their Sunday procession which symbolized the Risen Lord's triumphant return to Galilee. If there seems to be a feminine touch here, that is right: it was a church for women, who were warned by a line of marble in the nave floor to go no nearer to St Cuthbert's shrine. Here in 1370 they reburied the Venerable Bede, whose history of the conversion of Anglo-Saxon England tells us all that we know of St Cuthbert and of many other saints, including women.

In 1242 they tackled the east end again. The large east transept of Fountains Abbey in Yorkshire had suggested a solution to Durham's problem and Bishop Richard Poore, who had begun the new Salisbury Cathedral, had planned Durham's solution on his move there. With its floor almost 2 metres (6 feet) lower than the level of the choir, the large and lofty Chapel of the Nine Altars arose and was stable. Today its chief glory is the Joseph Window to the north (with tracery in two layers) and what is lacking is the nine altars. The joining of this work to the Norman choir makes a dramatic contrast. Today St Cuthbert's shrine is no more, but the screen between its site and the high altar has proved permanent in its delicate beauty. It was made in the London workshop of Henry Yevele, the architect of the Canterbury nave, and mostly paid for (in 1372) by a member of the great aristocratic house of Neville. Originally it included more than 100 alabaster statues. A bishop's throne, the highest in Christendom, was created by placing it on top of the monument which Bishop Hatfield was erecting for himself; he died in 1333. And the present central tower was begun in 1465. It is larger than, but inferior to, the older towers at the west end, for it lacks their ornamentation and its grandeur is slightly spoiled by the failure to remove the battlements erected at the top of the first stage before it was decided that the second stage could be afforded as a belfry.

The wealth of the cathedral after the closure of the monastery was derived partly from mining, which makes it especially appropriate that a memorial to miners was added in 1947. Other fine woodwork is found in the elaborate cover of the font and in what remains of the stalls. These survive from the gifts of Bishop John Cosin, who in the 1660s had to restore the cathedral after 4,000 Scottish prisoners, imprisoned here by Cromwell's army, had used what wood they could find as fuel. Other restoration took place under the Victorian clergy. They had to rectify earlier and clumsier attempts at conservation or improvement – including an attempt in the 1770s to cure the erosion of the exterior stone by shaving it, removing a few centimetres and not caring that the dimensions of the carving were destroyed. The Victorians, themselves masters of a kingdom and an empire, understood that Norman bishops and monks had told their masons to create overwhelming declarations of power and glory.

15 ELY

The 15th-century Tiptoft monument in Ely.

Ely Cathedral can be seen for mile after mile of flat emptiness and it must have looked even more like a ship before the Fens around it were drained in the 17th and 18th centuries. So where is the ship sailing to? In our time the 'city' of Ely is a quiet, small town in comparison with its neighbour Cambridge and for most of its history it was a village; its name means 'eel island'. Perhaps one may say that it is like a tug attending this church which is nothing less than a battleship of faith launched on a voyage to heaven.

A cathedral since 1109, and preserved from ruin by that fact, the church has not been a monastery since 1539. But only its monastic foundation can explain its size combined with its remoteness from what is called civilization. It was founded precisely in order to be remote, for Etheldreda, daughter of one king and wife of another, had refused to consummate either of her two marriages and had escaped to this island which she happened to own. Here she created a monastery with herself as abbess in 673. And here, after massacre and destruction by the Vikings, King Edgar of Wessex refounded the monastery in the Benedictine order in 970. A medieval song about King Canute claimed that he loved to hear the chants of the monks across the desolate waste of water. In our time the spirit of Ely is experienced best in an Evensong offered perfectly to the glory of God by a large choir and a small congregation on a winter's evening in an atmosphere of damp cold.

Apart from fragments such as part of a stone cross which was a memorial to Etheldreda's steward Ovin, the earliest part of the existing church is the south transept. With its richly-arcaded walls it is part of the work undertaken four centuries after Etheldreda by Abbot Simeon, a kinsman of William the Conqueror. He had been brought from Winchester (where his brother was bishop) to impose order on this remote island which had been the refuge of Anglo-Saxon rebels under Hereward the Wake. Using the hard Barnack limestone by permission of the monks of Peterborough, he rebuilt the church from the east end to this transept (now lightened by a Perpendicular window and a hammerbeam roof with painted angels).

In the next century the nave was finished, with three finely-sculptured doorways leading into it from the monks' cloister (now demolished). It is undeniably magnificent, owing much to its original proportions (the three storeys rise 6:5:4) and to the light entering through windows enlarged in later periods. One may feel dwarfed and oppressed by the relentless rhythm of this 26 metres (86 feet) high, almost 76 metres (250 feet) long and narrow nave, without any decoration apart from the fine painting on the wooden ceiling (done by two Victorian country gentlemen who did not charge). If so, one has a fellow-feeling with the Englishmen who were subjected to the Normans. The slightly later west end, one has to admit, is a welcome into the church. The front of the south-west transept has tracery in five storeys which become ever more adventurously exuberant as the eye travels up. The adjacent turret is almost jolly. Above it rises a tower of similar Late Norman or Transitional spirit. The Galilee porch is from the 13th century and looks positively happy to be free of the Norman yoke. Sadly, however, the north-west transept which matched the south-west one fell down in the 15th century. This may well have been caused by the erection of the octagonal belfry on top of the western tower – a structure which adds nothing to the appearance of this front. So the final impression left by the Norman work in Ely is, after all, one of power and wealth rather than beauty.

The bishops and monks in the Middle Ages certainly had power and wealth. One gathers that impression from the bishop's palace which was built about 1500 (and rebuilt in the 17th and 18th centuries), and from those buildings of the monastery which have survived as the houses of later clergy and the premises of the King's School. But beauty came into the cathedral when the east end was rebuilt by Bishop Hugh of Northwold between 1234 and 1254, to honour St Etheldreda's shrine. Its six bays were inspired by the nave of Lincoln and look like a dress rehearsal for the Angel Choir, although without any of Lincoln's figure sculpture; instead there are deeply-cut sprays of foliage. Alec Clifton-Taylor's *The Cathedrals of England* (1986) was unsentimental; in particular he had many reservations about Lincoln. But he called this part of Ely 'the most

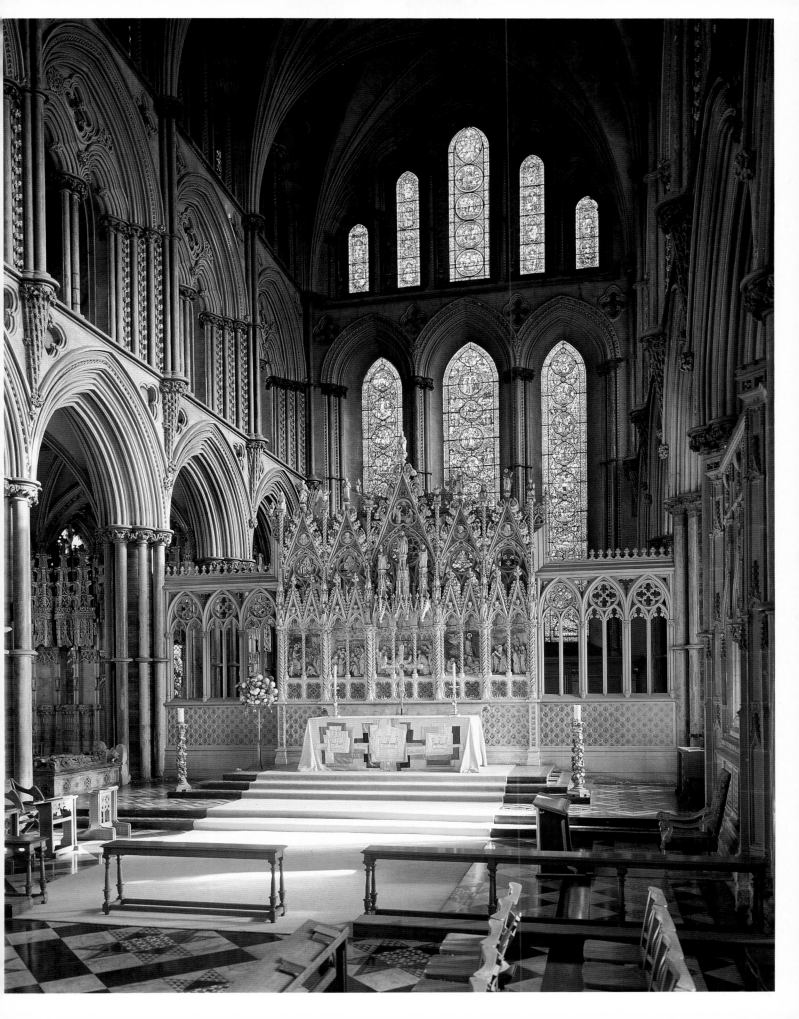

sumptuous example of Gothic architecture in England'.

All that was now wanted was a worthy Lady chapel and one was started in 1321. Since the church's straight east wall with its beautiful group of eight lancet windows had to stay, the chapel is a semi-detached building to the north-east. This room, which is a large parallelogram, is still breathtaking. Beneath the tracery of the now plain windows canopied seats for the monks are all round the walls. The stone vault, the widest in medieval England at 14 metres (46 feet), has many lierne ribs and innumerable bosses. But the original effect was incomparably richer. The windows and walls were full of colour which has now almost completely vanished. So were the many statues (carved in soft chalk) of saints and of scenes from Our Lady's legendary life, now savagely mutilated. The name of the master mason is lost, but the sacrist – the monk in charge of the fabric – is known to have been Alan of Walsingham. He had worked as a goldsmith.

Alan's was the mind that conceived the response to disaster when the Norman central tower collapsed in the very year after the beginning of the Lady chapel. There had been wooden octagonal towers in medieval churches before this, but on top of the stone towers: now this octagon was to have no floor. It became almost a dome, something unique in English Gothic architecture. The contrast is complete between the dark nave and the flood of light which comes diagonally from the large windows of the lantern and which compels one to look up to the vault – a star, twisted so that it sits differently from the ribs which seem to support it. And there is another striking contrast: between this superficial appearance and the structural reality, which is that the lantern is supported by a hidden miracle of carpentry (supervised by a master, William Hurley) including oak beams of 19 metres (63 feet) brought from Bedfordshire. Later

centuries have made 'restorations', often criticized by their successors; thus the external top of the octagon has often been thought too fussy as it now is, and the Victorian stained glass has been denounced, in Ely as elsewhere (although this cathedral defiantly provides a stained glass museum to instruct visitors). But the main reaction has been sheer wonder at the 14th-century feat of engineering.

Beneath the octagon, which has excellent acoustics, the monks worshipped in another Hurley masterpiece, the stalls, which have largely survived although moved nearer the high altar. The Norman bays of the crossing were rebuilt; and the arch at the east end of the nave is nothing less than tremendous. At the east end of the church chantry chapels commemorating Bishops Alcock and West showed the Perpendicular style floridly luxuriant at the end of the Middle Ages. They have survived as the largest of a series of memorials stretching across many centuries. But apart from these and other minor additions and alterations, the interior has remained virtually as it was in 1350. Ely needed nothing more – or such was the overwhelming impression, enabling successive generations to ignore the challenge of the reconstruction of the north-west transept.

Oliver Cromwell did not share Canute's enthusiasm for the chanting at Ely. He farmed as a tenant of the cathedral, but it is said that when he gained power he appeared with a troop of soldiers, expelled the clergy and choir and had the doors locked for 17 years. However, a respect for the sedately Anglican continuation of the monks' life has been a more normal reaction. And so Ely Cathedral has remained since the monks disappeared, although major repairs and reconstructions have often been necessary in order to make sure that their fabulous church did not disappear too, sunk in the ocean of time.

16 EXETER

The city of Exeter was heavily bombed in 1942, when the cathedral itself was hit — but the ugliness of much of the city's postwar rebuilding is not matched in the great church except in the choir-stalls in the nave. The bomb damage, from St James's chapel to the west window, has been lovingly made good in harmony with the medieval beauty of the rest. Exeter has some fine Georgian brick buildings including some in the Close, but there is very little of the 18th century in the cathedral itself apart from monuments which praise local worthies. And neither brick nor the local red sandstone is used in this church except between the ribs in the vault and in a few other small visible places, and in the rubble at the core of the walls. The grey limestone comes from the quarry in Beer.

What can truthfully be said to be typical of Devon in this cathedral is the common sense: it does not soar high; there is no mystery. We are solidly on good earth between Somerset's dreams about Arthur's kingdom of Avalon and Cornwall's memories of Celtic saints as unearthly as the ocean's spray. In this cathedral the arches are made of a sandstone with the colour of cream and much of the stone has recently been repainted with the colours of the Devon countryside – red, green and sun-like gold. The monuments of generations of bishops and knights seem to bring the comfortable wealth of manor houses into this museum of a county's pride, but bosses and corbels almost as good as the carving in Southwell's chapter house show a keen observation of the wealth of nature – rose and vine, oak, ivy and hawthorn – and in the Lady chapel there are two lovely wood carvings which are more homely than aristocratic. In one the Virgin Mary is being given an apple by her mother. In the other shepherds and sheep are enjoying the first Christmas. The first tablet one sees on entering the north-west porch is a memorial to Richard Blackmore, fruit farmer and author of the Victorian bestseller *Lorna Doone: A Romance of Exmoor* (1869).

Because the main road into Devon crosses the river Exe, this has been a place of religious as well as political importance since Roman times. A small church existed here for more than 300 years before Canute repaired and endowed it in 1019. The bishop was moved here from Crediton in 1050 and given a diocese

which included Cornwall – a rare piece of ecclesiastical reorganization before the Normans came. The Normans did come and the great church which was built during the 12th century (1112-60) had twin towers at the ends of the transepts. These have rightly been admired ever since. When Walter Bronescombe, who became Bishop of Exeter in 1258, determined to rebuild his cathedral in a style which would match Salisbury's (whose consecration he probably witnessed five months after his enthronement), these towers had to be preserved externally. Their insides were turned into short transepts. The conservatism which he displayed in this matter commended itself to Devon and was equalled by his successors in the bishopric. With only minor variations they maintained the style which was established in the Lady chapel, completed shortly after his death. So just as Salisbury is consistently Early English, Exeter is all Decorated. The vault is no more than 21 metres (69 feet) high in order to avoid eclipsing the towers, but it is over 91 metres (300 feet) long and no Gothic vault anywhere is longer. The name of its architect is unknown.

Externally the cathedral is nothing special apart from the towers. The cloister has gone and the chapter house is unremarkable. The

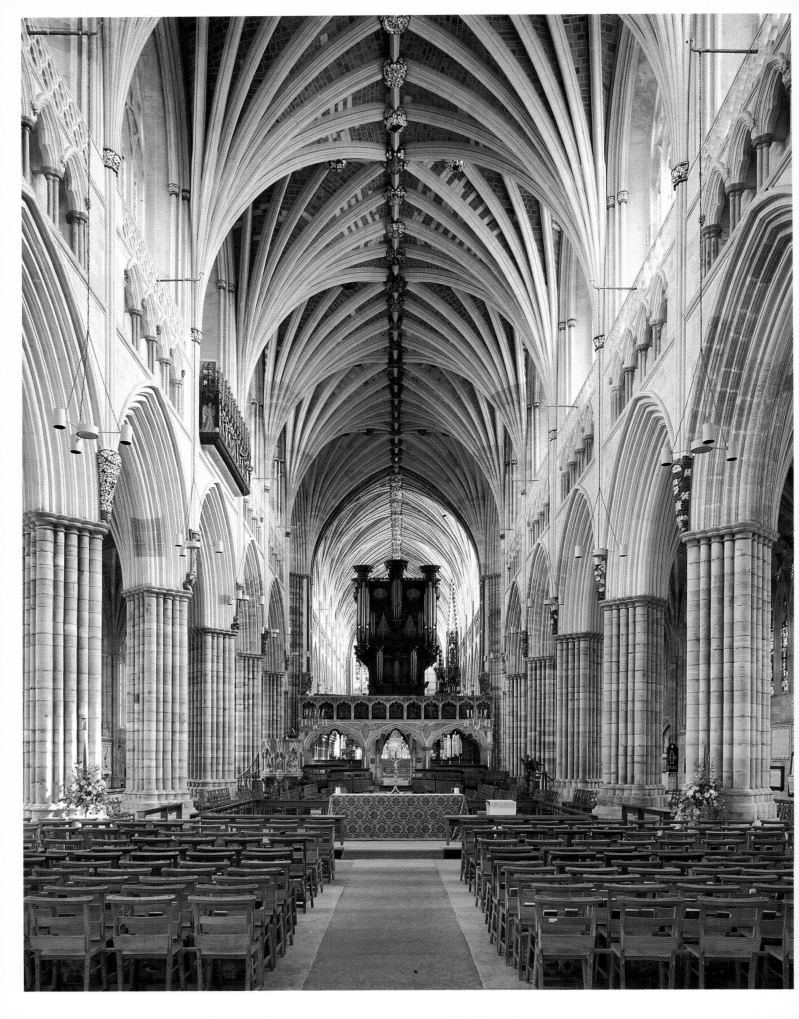

west front is inconsequential in comparison with Wells or Lincoln. The three storeys are unrelated to each other. At the top a window peeps out above a battlement and at the bottom the screen, filled with statues, is an afterthought which obscures the three windows. Many of the kings (of Judah or England?) sit in cross-legged conversation and seem unaware of the fact that they have lost their colour and crumbled gently since about 1375. Above them charming small figures play in the battlements, but these seem to be of the 15th century – yet another afterthought.

One has to go inside and look down the cathedral. Here one appreciates the advantage of there being no central tower, for one sees what a unified glory could be achieved by the Decorated style when it was disciplined. Alec Clifton-Taylor rightly praised this as one of 'the supreme architectural pleasures of England'.

The piers of the 14 bays are of unpolished Purbeck 'marble', mostly soft grey but slightly tinted with other colours. The sandstone of the pointed arches has been moulded like these piers, so that, although some Norman masonry was used again when the cathedral was reconstructed, there is absolutely no hint of Norman massiveness. There is also no gallery of Norman dimensions. In the earlier stages of the rebuilding no triforium was envisaged, but it was decided to add one, a muted version of the arcade below. The vaulting springs up from the carved and painted corbels on top of the piers. This makes all the 16 ribs seem necessary to the structure, but that is only an illusion. As they branch out – and the comparison with an avenue of palm trees is inescapable – almost all of these ribs have no job to do except to be beautiful. As they meet the ribs springing from the opposite arcade there is, so to speak, a final shout of joy – a long row of painted and gilded bosses. In the middle of the south side is a minstrels' gallery. When no human singers or trumpeters are present, 14 stone angels playing musical instruments including a bagpipe seem to carry on the happy noise. On one of the corbels carved above the main arcade a tumbler does a trick.

John Grandisson thoroughly deserves his little chantry chapel tucked into the west wall. He was Bishop of Exeter for more than 40 years, 1327-69, and despite the Black Death he saw this marvellous building through to completion. His master mason was Thomas of Witney until about 1342. From Bronescombe's east to Grandisson's west took almost 100 years.

There are many things to admire beneath this vault. One of them is a set of 48 misericords (the oldest complete set in the country) carved beneath the stalls of the 24 canons and their deputies in the 1250s. These survived both the destruction of the Norman cathedral in which they were placed at first and the destruction of the later medieval stalls in Protestant days. The stalls which we see are by Gilbert Scott, part of his extensive restoration when the cathedral had to be consoled for the loss of Cornwall to the new diocese of Truro in 1877. The east window has preserved some lovely glass painted in 1303-04 by Master Walter, the first English glazier whose work we can identify; and the tracery in all the windows shows many ingenious variations in geometry, although each window in the south wall corresponds with one in the north.

Two canopies made by carpenters in the 1310s are towering masterpieces of craftsmanship. One is over the set of stone *sedilia* (clergy seats) near the high altar and the other rises high above the bishop's throne in Devon oak. The *pulpitum* was made a few years later with equal but more sober craftsmanship. Like the throne it was commissioned by Bishop Stapledon, the unpopular minister of Edward II; he was murdered like his royal master. The *pulpitum* is of the see-through type, with room for two altars. Above it are two additions of the 17th century – a row of biblical pictures and a large organ case. There is even some Perpendicular work in Exeter Cathedral: a fan vault in the north-west porch, windows and roof in the chapter house, the battlements and pinnacles of the Norman towers and the top storey of the north tower which housed the bell, Great Peter.

A 15th-century clock face in the north transept is a good reminder that the days in which such a cathedral was created were timeless in comparison with the modern age. The medieval work shows only the hours (although an 18th-century dial adds the minutes) and the moon and the sun revolve around the earth. The moon revolves on its own axis to show its phases, but it is all much simpler than the navigational calculations which were to make Devon men the sailors of the world's oceans.

17 GLOUCESTER

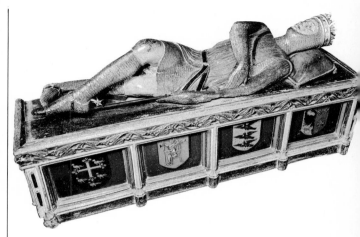

It is fitting that the exhibition housed since 1981 in the Norman gallery which runs round the choir of Gloucester Cathedral should have royal patronage as a theme, for this great church which traces its foundation to 681 does indeed owe much to kings. (Perhaps sheep should also have been featured, for much of the medieval monastery's wealth was derived from its ownership of at least 10,000 sheep.) When Henry VIII made it a cathedral in 1541 he referred to 'the monument of our renowned ancestor', Edward II. Had that royal 'martyr' not been buried here so splendidly and so profitably, the abbey of Gloucester might well have had a history more like St Albans: never fully modernized after its Norman construction and doomed to decay when the monks left. As it was, many of the neighbouring churches which gave rise to the medieval proverb 'as sure as God's in Gloucester' were demolished or neglected. Nowadays Gloucester is an industrial town, possessing Europe's largest ice cream factory. Although still full of interest it is compared by visitors with Cheltenham, Tewkesbury and Worcester – and not to its advantage. But under royal patronage the great church in the city's centre has been through many centuries a stronghold of English religion and history.

The strategic position of Gloucester, where the old road from London and Oxford to Hereford and Wales crossed the Severn, made it a Roman garrison town and centuries later caused both Mercia and Wessex to secure it as a frontier town for their kingdoms, with a modest royal palace. The Normans built a strong castle here. Next to it was St Peter's abbey, which according to tradition had been founded by King Osric in 681. But the abbey began to thrive only when the Conqueror's chaplain Serlo was appointed abbot. Under his rule the numbers of the monks rose from two to a hundred and a new church also rose, using stone from the local quarry in Painswick. Of this, the low crypt remains but has needed reinforcements because of the increasing weight of what later generations did to Serlo's church above it. The towers of the transepts and the two chapels radiating off the ambulatory of the choir still give some idea of what the church looked like in its new beginning. The nave was mostly built after

Serlo's death in 1104 and a lead font now in the Lady chapel is not much later.

Although the nave is almost as plain as the crypt, the twelve high and huge cylinders which are the Norman pillars are majestic, supporting an oddly small triforium. The clerestory and vault which look separate are work of the 1240s, replacing a disastrously fire-prone wooden ceiling. The vault is too low and too plain and the report in the abbey's chronicle that the monks built it themselves may refer to a dispute they had with the masons during this disappointing project – although one suspects that had the monks really done everything themselves their work would have been clumsier still. The heaviness of this vault meant that Abbot Thokey had to rebuild the wall of the south aisle in the 1320s. The masons he used did it in the Geometric style then familiar, peppering it with the fashionable ball-flower ornamentation which also proliferates on the spire of Salisbury. The two western bays and the façade of the nave, with the south porch leading into it, had to be rebuilt about a century later in the Perpendicular style. Presumably the intention was to redo the whole nave in Perpendicular when funds permitted. As things were, a dramatic improvement in the monastery's finances did not extend to that.

Abbot Wigmore was the man who hired the masons who introduced the Perpendicular style, taking splendid advantage of the burial of Edward II. In life this king had been despised by the barons and modern historians have not

been much kinder to him. ('Our sources afford us no evidence', wrote that stern historian May McKisack in her volume in the *Oxford History of England*, 'that at any time he tried to rise to his responsibilities or to learn from his misfortunes and mistakes'.) He had been murdered in Berkeley Castle at the instigation of his queen and her lover. Abbot Thokey has been called brave to offer burial to such an outcast, but Gloucester had already been favoured as the place to honour borderline royalty. Robert Curthose, the eldest son of the Conqueror, was bequeathed the duchy of Normandy rather than the kingdom of England. Having quarrelled with his more favoured brothers William II and Henry I, he had been imprisoned in Cardiff Castle for 28 years. But his body had been brought to Gloucester in 1134 and a century and a half later he had received the honour of a painted effigy in oak with military dress of that later period. (In the 1640s this effigy was broken up by the Parliamentarians but the pieces were rescued by a Royalist squire.) When burying Edward II Abbot Thokey acted on the orders of those who guarded the young Edward III and received essential assistance from them. They arranged the lavish funeral and the tomb, where a three-pinnacled canopy surmounts an alabaster effigy. And as a reward for co-operation they supplied large grants and royal masons when the monastery embarked on the modernization of the transepts and choir.

The 14th-century work began and ended in the transepts: from the south in 1331 to the north in 1374. Since it was the first great achievement in the Perpendicular style, its story has already been told in outline (pages 58-60). Gloucester Cathedral forces the admission that English art lost something when Decorated splendour went out, for the tomb of Edward II and the intricate vault of the choir are two masterpieces of stonemasons working in that style and the carpenters showed what beauty they could create in the choir stalls. But the simplification of stone carving made it possible for thousands of churches to be built or rebuilt in Perpendicular even after the Black Death and during the Wars of the Roses. That would never have been possible if it had been thought necessary to develop Decorated into a flamboyance even more costly in skill and money.

In addition to the transformation of the transepts and the choir (with flying buttresses across the ambulatory, to support the weight of the choir's new vault and then the new tower), there are four other Perpendicular masterpieces in this church.

The east window seems to have been finished by 1357 while the country was beginning to recover from the terrible first impact of the Black Death. It has 14 lights, measures 24 metres (80 feet) by 11.5 metres (38 feet) and curves outwards in a slight bow. The yellow stain on the glass enables portraiture in the Coronation of the Virgin and in the almost life-sized figures of apostles, saints, kings, bishops and abbots. The bubbles in the plain glass make it silvery and lighten the display of these figures and of the heraldic shields which are thought to provide clues to the window's origins. One of the shields belonged to Lord Bradeston, who is believed to have been the donor. Another commemorates his friend Sir Maurice Berkeley, killed during the siege of Calais in 1347. Like eight other knights whose shields are here they had fought together in the battle of Crécy, the decisive moment in Edward III's conquest of France. So this immense window is a war memorial from the age of chivalry, when soldiers laid their valiant deeds at the feet of the crowned Virgin. In comparison with, say, Wells or York, the glass is dull — but it can be seen as an expression of patriotism even further than any expression intended in the Middle Ages. For the effect is of red, white and blue.

The reconstruction of the cloister, the finest in England, was started with the east 'walk' on the orders of Abbot Horton, who reigned 1351-77. Each of its four walks is slightly different; the work was not finished until 1412. Almost as interesting as the fan vaulting which made its first appearance here is a series of reminders that the monks had a domestic life. The upper lights of the windows were glazed for comfort in the 14th century although the existing glass was inserted when the cathedral had long ceased to be a monastery. There are 20 miniature studies where the monks read and wrote and a *lavatorium* under a smaller fan vault where they washed. Cuts in the stone enable the experts to tell what games the young novices played. Through this cloister one enters the chapter house which is mostly of the 12th century. It may be the room in which the Conqueror ordered Domesday Book to be compiled; we know that he held the decisive council in Gloucester. The more elaborate east end was added in the 15th century, almost 100 years after the construction of the library which is another room echoing with history.

The tower, 68.5 metres (225 feet) high, was built on the Norman base in the middle of the 15th century, when victories in France were being replaced by civil wars at home. Patterned by tracery and crowned by a parapet and by pinnacles, it leaves no doubt about the power of the Perpendicular style to affirm confidence, whatever clouds may be in the nation's sky; and here hangs England's only great bell surviving from the Middle Ages. The monk

called Tully, who is recorded as the architect of this marvellous tower, achieved something that was at least the rival of the tower of his diocese's cathedral, in Worcester.

The Lady chapel was finished in the 1490s as the last triumph of the Gloucester masons in the Perpendicular style which had served them so well over some 170 years. It is semi-detached at the east end, in order to reduce the shadow on the east window. On either side are chantry chapels, with galleries above which are still sometimes used by the cathedral choir. Like the Decorated Lady chapel in Ely, this marvellous little church has been defaced by religious fanaticism and here one suspects the influence of Bishop Hooper, the ultra-Protestant who was burned at the stake not far away during the Roman Catholic reaction under Queen Mary, in 1555. Only medieval scribbling in the empty niches above the altar shows where statues stood in the Middle Ages (although modern tapestry occupies three niches now) and only jumbled fragments show how good was the glass which once filled these great windows; almost all the old glass to be seen now came from windows elsewhere. But the brilliantly intricate vault is still in position.

After the Reformation Gloucester Cathedral – as it now was – escaped the worst. The tomb built for the last abbot was used by two bishops. Communion rails in the Lady chapel come from the time when William Laud, then dean but later Charles I's archbishop, was restoring dignity in Anglican worship, and the choir-stalls and bishop's throne now in the nave come from early in the 18th century, often regarded as a time when all dignity had disappeared. The medieval *pulpitum* has gone but the stone screen which replaced it in 1820 is harmless and the fine organ case above it comes from the time when Charles II was restored to the throne of his fathers. The extensive Victorian restoration is less criticized here than in some other cathedrals, the reredos over the high altar being particularly successful. In the 1950s all the roofs were renewed and since then the church has been filled with colour and life. Visiting it, one senses that some of the beauty of God is visible in Gloucester Cathedral.

18 HEREFORD

One reason why Hereford Cathedral seems so English is obvious: the border with the Black Mountains of Wales is so close. But there are more subtle reasons. It can be compared with, say, Chichester because its most prominent feature — here a tower not a spire — rises above a pleasant scene of country and town, yet is unobtrusive. The view from across the Wye, with the bishop's lawn sweeping down to the river from his pink-grey cathedral, is the old English tradition pictured. And life in this market town remains unhurried. The diocese of Hereford has been agricultural ever since its foundation (about 676) and after seeing the orchards one is not surprised to find that Bulmers, the cider firm, recently restored the cathedral organ. The 15th-century Wyclif Bible preserved here refers to 'cidir' instead of wine.

Hereford Cathedral is also English in the courage in rebuilding after disasters. Such courage is, of course, not the monopoly of any nation. The history of Wales is full of it and this book began with the brave story of Llandaff Cathedral. But in some of the history of this border country ('the Marches') courage has been needed on both sides. The fortified bridge in Monmouth is a reminder of this. In the ecclesiastical world there were many disputes about whether parishes should be in a Welsh or English diocese. And although the Welsh and the English have made peace, time has inflicted decay on buildings such as this cathedral which have used the local sandstone.

Probably Hereford's first stone church was built when Ethelbert, King of East Anglia, was buried here in 792. Both his murder and his burial far from his followers had been ordered by Offa, the mighty King of Mercia. Hereford Cathedral has been dedicated to St Ethelbert as well as to the Virgin Mary ever since. Bishop Athelstan built a bigger Saxon church, only to have it burned by the Welsh. In the 11th century a Norman cathedral replaced it, and was used as the headquarters of an army siding with Matilda against Stephen's garrison in Hereford Castle in the civil war of the 1140s. In later centuries of peace the Norman work seemed unworthy and many alterations were made, including the addition of a fine west tower. But this tower crashed down in 1786, destroying much of the nave. The lead roof of the ten-sided chapter house had been used to

The shrine of St Thomas Cantilupe in Hereford.

make bullets for the Royalists in the civil war of the 1640s and the whole house, having been used as a quarry, was demolished in 1769 although its fan vaulting, made in the 1360s, was the second oldest in England. Centuries of erosion meant that most of the stonework of the east end had to be renewed by the Victorian restorers, Lewis Cottingham and Sir George Gilbert Scott. In brief, what we see today is a cathedral built by responses to political and natural challenges which we might not expect to occur in a countryside which nowadays seems so deeply calm. And in the 1980s repairs to the fabric have again become urgent.

Hereford Cathedral has many points of interest although none of these is spectacular. The Norman piers remain in the nave; in his *Cathedral Architecture* (1972) Hugh Braun reckoned them 'perhaps the most successful treatment of the circular pillar in English architecture'. But everything above them is the work of James Wyatt in the 1790s and the painted vault is of timber. In the south transept one wall is full of Norman arcading and two others frame great Perpendicular windows above a Norman fireplace. The north transept has a wall which more or less copies Westminster Abbey.

Hereford Cathedral, much restored after the decay of sandstone.

Where music is offered in Hereford Cathedral.

It was planned by Bishop Peter de Aquablanca (an Italian favoured by Henry III) who had watched that abbey being built. When he died in 1268, he was buried here. A few feet away is the first tomb of Thomas Cantilupe, a very different character – a scholarly and pastoral bishop, the friend and ally of Simon de Montfort. He died in 1282. The cathedral's medieval fortune was made by Thomas, that good and English man, who was far more popular than Aquablanca. His tomb is carved with mourning knights. When the Pope canonized him in 1320, his body was transferred to a splendid shrine (now gone) in the Lady chapel.

At last Hereford had a saint more interesting than St Ethelbert and the pilgrims came with money. The Lady chapel had already been rebuilt in the Early English style (about 1230), but there was now both need and opportunity for new aisles and new eastern transepts, as the pilgrims' way to the shrine. The canons treated themselves to a remodelling of the chancel, to new stalls in it (with good misericords) and finally to the two towers. Of these the central one has survived from about 1310 although the top belongs to the 19th century.

There is not much Decorated ornamentation apart from the west front – which is in fact the unfortunate attempt of John Oldrid Scott in the 1900s to build what he thought the Middle Ages ought to have built. (The medieval front was plain Norman before the now vanished Perpendicular west tower arose.) But there is some good Perpendicular, including the fan-vaulted chantry chapel of Bishop Stanbury who was Henry VI's agent in the foundation of Eton College. Since 1475 the Vicars' Cloisters have preserved a timbered domesticity. They were built for 27 vicars who sang the services. If we wonder how this comparatively poor cathedral could afford such a staff, one explanation is that they had the right to take (and charge for) all the funerals in the city and in the villages for some miles around.

The clergy of Hereford Cathedral have at times made it a seat of learning and the chief evidence in praise of medieval scholarship is still on view in the cathedral. There is a library of almost 1,450 old books, chained to discourage thieves: the largest chained library in the world. The books include copies of gospels and of the *Anglo-Saxon Chronicle* dating from the 9th century. From the 12th and 13th centuries 144 books remain, including the *Hereford Breviary* which shows the music sung here in about 1270.

The cathedral exhibits a map of the world made at about the same time as the service book. Presumably a visual aid once used in teaching, it is practically an encyclopaedia of geography and legend (containing more of the

In the north transept of Hereford this wall built in the 1260s reproduced the style of the new royal abbey in Westminster.

latter than of the former), claiming to be based on the 5th-century work of Orosius, but incorporating much that was reckoned general knowledge in the map-maker's own day. We are given the name of the maker, for in Norman French he asks us to pray for him: he was Richard of Haldingham and Lafford. Almost certainly this refers to a priest, Richard de Bello, who was a canon of Lincoln Cathedral in 1264-83 with a prebend derived from those two villages. (A Richard de Bello was in the company of the Bishop of Hereford in 1289, but it is far from clear that he was the same man.) Either he or a scribe whom he used made strange errors in the Latin as well as in the geography; Africa is labelled as Europe. The map is fascinating, not least because it puts Jerusalem at the centre of the world and the islands of Britain and Ireland on the edge, as remote as Ceylon. One suddenly realizes that a medieval priest in England did feel that he was

poverty hidden away), propagate the challenging ideals of Christian internationalism. And the beauty of this place has a message for people everywhere.

Thomas Traherne, the son of a Hereford cobbler, was rector of the village of Credenhill for ten years from 1657. His *Centuries of Meditation* were left in a notebook until bought for a few pence from a barrow in 1895. They recall the city of his childhood and express for all time what a cathedral is meant to say about the dignity of people. 'The men! O what venerable and reverend creatures did the aged seem! And young men glittering and sparkling angels, and maids strange Seraphic pieces of life and beauty! Boys and girls tumbling in the street, and playing, were moving jewels'.

And Traherne also put into words what this decaying but restored structure of ancient stone says about God's world. He told a parishioner that she must see 'how a sand exhibiteth the wisdom and power of God . . . You will never enjoy the world aright, till the sea itself floweth in your veins, till you are clothed with the heavens and crowned with the stars . . . till you are familiar with the ways of God in all ages as with your walk and table'.

That is the timeless message of Hereford.

sitting on the world's rim. But one of his tasks was to connect a rural and remote island with the events which had made Jerusalem central. In our own time the diocese and cathedral of Hereford, while properly encouraging study and action about local problems (for there is

19 LICHFIELD

The Sleeping Children in Lichfield by Sir Francis Chantry.

The brick-and-lawn Georgian attractiveness of Lichfield, in the agriculturally calm valley of the Trent between the Black Country and the Potteries, has escaped the stresses both of industry and of tourism. Essentially it is still the town where Samuel Johnson grew up as a bookseller's son. Those who do discover these charms keep in their memory the image of the three spires ('the Ladies of the Vale') rising above the two great pools and the Close, which has been an ecclesiastical village since the 13th century and although not very large is full of good houses. In recent years a festival each summer has been at the centre of imaginative efforts to make this cathedral more widely known, but at present part of the beauty is the fact that not everyone is aware that this is the most historic shrine in the centre of England.

Peace is one's first and last impression, yet the history of Lichfield is far from tranquil. There is a tradition that 1,000 Christians were martyred here during the persecution ordered by the emperor Diocletian – which may explain Lichfield's name (it means 'field of the dead') and why George Fox, the founder of the Quakers, rode through the place crying 'Woe to the bloody city!'. That was in the 17th century, when there had just been large-scale violence locally. During two sieges, in 1643 and 1646, not only the Close but the cathedral itself formed a Royalist stronghold and both were literally bombarded. The medieval windows were shattered; the woodwork, books and records were burned; the tombs were rifled and smashed; the lead was stripped from the roof; the central spire was shot down. After 1662 Bishop Hacket repaired most of that damage, much of the work being done at his own expense. On the west front he substituted a statue of Charles II for one of Christ in Majesty. But during the 18th century no more work on the decaying fabric of this church built of red sandstone was attempted, until the 1790s, when James Wyatt was commissioned to save the nave from collapsing outwards by removing most of the stone vault.

All the energy of the Victorians was needed to conserve and reconstruct, often improving on the clumsy restorations by their predecessors. It was a dramatic part of the revival and expansion of the Victorian Church. Victorian energy is memorialized also in the tomb of the

first Anglican bishop of New Zealand, George Augustus Selwyn, Bishop of Lichfield for ten years from 1868. He rests here amid scenes of Maori life finely depicted on tiles made by William de Morgan. The restoration of the cathedral was led by the Gilbert Scotts, father Sir George and son John Oldrid, between 1857 and the end of the century. They added their own firm touches from end to end – from the west front which was now virtually all new, to the high altar with a superb pavement in front of it. The painted iron screen between choir and nave and the iron and brass pulpit near it are nothing less than magnificent. And the 20th century has continued to care for the fabric at considerable expense.

If we peer further back into history we find that Bishops Hacket and Selwyn were only two of a long line of bishops who have had to struggle to make Lichfield a centre of church life. The story goes back to the foundation in 700 of a small church around the tomb of St Chad, who before his death in 672 had been bishop for less than three years. Like St Cuthbert in the north, Chad became a symbol of unity in the Christian mission to an England still largely pagan. Trained on the Holy Island of Lindisfarne and willing to be made Bishop of York while the existing bishop, St Wilfrid, was absent abroad, he nevertheless accepted Catholic customs, and agreed to retire from the York bishopric to his little monastery at Lastingham on the Yorkshire moors. When summoned to do another brief spell as a bishop, this time in the kingdom of Mercia, he charmed everyone by his humility. When Mercia became both Christian and politically dominant there were Archbishops of Lichfield

The west front of Lichfield has needed much restoration.

Lichfield Cathedral uniquely has three spires.

for a few years (786-803); but here was no rival to Canterbury, York or indeed Lincoln. St Chad was venerated by pilgrims until the Reformation but his successors had to administer a diocese which sprawled with no obvious centre.

The Normans, thinking Lichfield too small, based the bishop first at Chester and then at Coventry. In 1239 an agreement was reached: the abbot and monks of Coventry and the dean and canons of Lichfield were to elect their bishop jointly. It was called the diocese of 'Lichfield and Coventry' until 1836. Gradually it has been reduced in extent but it is still a big diocese with a large, and mostly industrial, population. Black pollution has marked the cathedral permanently – and it is industrial Birmingham that now claims ownership of some of the bones of St Chad (in the Roman Catholic cathedral).

Despite these problems the cathedral was built grandly. Its clergy were organized and endowed in the 12th century although very little of the church built for them is still visible. Three bays of the Early English choir begun at the end of that century are still the heart of the church. That new start was followed by the present transepts and chapter house, finished by 1240. The nave and central tower rose next, very graceful in the geometric phase of the Decorated style. The 14th century contributed the west spires and the Lady chapel, which is as lofty as the rest of the cathedral, with nine tall windows (now filled with glass made in Flanders in two periods of the 16th century). Then came the job of joining the Lady chapel

to the choir. It was not easy because the cathedral had been built with a slight curve – either through an error in surveying or because it rests on a curving crag of rocks – but the architectural problems were solved with brilliant success by the master mason William Ramsey, who elsewhere seems to have more or less invented the Perpendicular style. In Lichfield the only Perpendicular features are some windows added in the 15th century.

The final impression, then, is one of peace. If the spires 'do not aspire' (as Pevsner said) it is because they are of uneven heights – 78.5 metres (258 feet) and 60 metres (193 feet) – and are not tall in relation to a fairly long and much ornamented building. Nor are these spires slender. They seem to say that here is a church built not of aspirations but of Midlands sandstone. What is most eloquent in the cathedral now speaks of peace, not struggle, and of innocence, not privilege. The last emblem of the Close's walled and fortified separation disappeared when the big gateway was pulled down in 1800. Inside the cathedral, the best-loved monument is of two little girls, Canon Robinson's daughters, who died in 1812. Their mother commissioned Sir Francis Chantry to sculpt them asleep. It is sentimental, but no parent can be untouched by seeing them or by reading beneath them: 'of such is the kingdom of God'. And in the chapter house is a richly decorated copy of the gospels made about 730 on the island of Lindisfarne. It was hidden during the violence of the 1640s, and is a precious link across turbulent centuries with the peaceable holiness of Chad.

John Ruskin's Victorian tribute to 'the most precious piece of architecture in the British Isles' seems right, if one is thinking about medieval architecture at any rate. Lincoln Cathedral is a giant. York Minster is larger but here the site is more spectacular and the architects were more imaginative. The size of the cathedral (as of York Minster) is partly explained by the dimensions of its diocese in the Middle Ages. This stretched from the Humber to the Thames in Oxfordshire at that time and only in 1884 was it restricted to Lincolnshire. The immensity of the diocese also explains why in the Middle Ages there were 53 canons or prebendaries (mostly non-resident) plus their 'vicars' and other assistant clergy. In comparison with York, Lincoln suffers from the deterioration of the stone on this exposed site and from a smaller number of visitors. During the winter its vast spaces have only pockets of heat. But recent generations have repaired this cathedral energetically and although it now has less medieval glass than York, its collection of Victorian glass is the best in Britain.

The Romans built an important town at the crossroads of what is now Lincoln but if there was a Roman cathedral no trace of it has been found. St Paulinus, the missionary bishop to this part of Anglo-Saxon England, did not make his base here. The Danes came and the bishop of the time moved as far away from them as possible, to Dorchester-on-Thames. So the known history begins with the arrival of Remigius as the first Norman bishop in 1072. Using limestone mainly from the local quarry of Ancaster a cathedral was built near the castle, with a wooden roof which caught fire. It was rebuilt by Bishop Alexander the Magnificent in the 1140s with a stone vault which caused it to collapse during an earthquake on Palm Sunday 1185. In addition to the black stone font made in Belgium (like Winchester's), what survives from this period is at the west end, in the nave and the façade. The work is inevitably plain but some sculptures of about 1145 have remained which broadcast the magnificent bishop's message to his diocese. Their style seems to be connected with the west fronts being made at about the same time for St Denis in France and for Modena Cathedral in Italy. The pleasures of the

The 14th-century south transept of Lincoln with the 'Bishop's Eye' window.

blessed and the torments of the damned are depicted educationally. So are relevant scenes from the Old Testament, where Adam and Eve are expelled from Paradise but Noah and Daniel escape damnation by obedience.

Above and around the Norman work later builders erected an enormous façade, similarly intended to impress. But across more than 53 metres (175 feet) the craftsmen of the 1240s repeated the tracery so often and so dully that, as Pevsner notes, the effect is 'curious rather than beautiful'. When heightening the central doorway the men of the 14th century destroyed the unifying sculpture of Christ in Majesty and substituted a frieze of 11 bearded and seated kings. And there was to be no visual connection between this façade and the splendid western towers built in the next century on their Norman base. Inside the cathedral a strengthening wall had to be built in the 18th century.

We owe the beginning of the Lincoln tradition of excellence to St Hugh of Avalon. A Burgundian nobleman's son, he was a scholar

The Angel Choir of Lincoln, built between 1256 and 1280, was so named from the 28 angels looking down on the high altar and the shrine of St Hugh.

PSALMS

HYMNS

and a man of God who had been the prior of an exceptionally austere monastery in Somerset (a 'Charterhouse'). Perhaps because of his wit, of which a few specimens are recorded, he was Henry II's only close friend among the bishops. Because of his pastoral work he was also loved in his diocese. Among his interests was an appreciation of new architecture, so that when he began the rebuilding of his cathedral in 1192 he employed a master mason, Geoffrey de Noiers, who was more radically and riskily innovative than William of Sens had been in Canterbury a few years before. The early *Metrical Life of St Hugh* says that this great bishop's enthusiasm extended to working on the building 'with the sweat of his own brow' as he 'often bore the hod-load of hewn stone'.

He must often have had to defend the architect from critics, for St Hugh's choir and the great transepts which have six chapels are undeniably provocative. The irregular, non-functional tiercerons in the vaulting have frequently been called crazy. Thick walls with only small buttresses take the strain of the vault's weight. In the aisles and parts of the transepts the arcading has not one but two planes. Here as elsewhere Purbeck 'marble' (or its more accessible equivalent from Alwalton) is used plentifully and playfully and the carving of foliage ('stiff leaf') on the capitals is deep and crisp. It seems from excavations that the rest of the east end of the church, the part which was soon to be demolished, was no less extraordinary. It had seven radiating chapels with irregular shapes in addition to two small

extra transepts and two larger chapels.

After the death of this eccentric genius (about 1220) other master masons built more soberly. In the transepts the arcading no longer had double planes. In the south transept a Galilee porch had purposes similar to the Galilee chapel in Durham, and in the north transept a rose window had 'plate' tracery and good glass (which has survived in this 'Dean's Eye'). In the nave the vault is broad – almost 30 metres (100 feet) – and it again has tiercerons without a practical purpose, but their star pattern pleases easily. Inevitably a comparison is made between this nave and the almost contemporary choir of Canterbury. The comparison shows that Purbeck or Alwalton 'marble' is used more lavishly here and helps to establish many more vertical lines. But no attempt is made to concentrate on height. The six arches are much wider than Canterbury's, the piers have three different patterns and there are two lancet windows in each bay of the aisle. The triforium is richly decorated and the clerestory is also elaborate, with two arches in each bay here also. In short, the eyes are invited to feast on the walls rather than to speed upwards.

Demolition followed, some accidental when the central tower collapsed in the 1230s, some deliberate when pilgrims to St Hugh's tomb became so numerous that the decision was taken to pull down the east end of the cathedral which he had rebuilt. Between 1256 and 1280 it was replaced by the Angel Choir, so named from the 28 angels who adorn the triforium,

116

some with musical instruments, some occupied in the sterner tasks of judgment. The work appears to have been inspired by the new Westminster Abbey although the choir of Ely is also slightly older than this Decorated splendour in Lincoln. The arches are 1.5 metres (5 feet) narrower than in the nave and the decoration of the triforium between the unforgettable angels is still more sumptuous. The clerestory has its own decoration on the back wall as well as at the front and the bosses in the vault are Britain's best of this date, with some naturalistic foliage. And there is a great east window, now with glass of 1855. In the 13th century the masons also built a ten-sided chapter house, a cloister, elaborate doorways leading from the nave to the aisles of the choirs, and porches which beckoned pilgrims into the Angel Choir from the outside world. In these noble portals Westminster Abbey was again the inspiration and as in Westminster much of the medieval sculpture has had to be replaced because of the erosion of the stone. On the south side the Judgment Porch repeats the warnings carved on Alexander the Magnifi-cent's west front 140 years before. The outside world is a world under condemnation.

The 14th century brought further enrichments to Lincoln Cathedral, itself an embodiment of the Church's gospel of salvation. About 1300 an Easter Sepulchre was added to the Angel Choir. The stone carving of its six bays is exquisitely delicate. On the left was the tomb of a bishop (Remigius?). On the right, above sculptured soldiers asleep by Christ's tomb, was the place where the Body of Christ (in the sacrament) was brought on Maundy Thursday, to rest until early on Easter Day. Almost as fine are the finely-decorated *pulpitum* separating the choir from the nave, the flowing tracery in the south transept window (called the Bishop's Eye) and the canopied stalls in oak for the clergy.

In a very different architectural triumph, the height of the central tower was raised to 82.5 metres (271 feet) and the spire above it was the highest in medieval Britain. Above a new west window the two west towers were raised during the 15th century to a height only 18 metres (60 feet) less and they, too, had spires (until 1807).

The usual tale of destruction and neglect followed the arrival of Protestantism, but in 1674 Sir Christopher Wren rebuilt the north wall of the cloister and added a library above it to house Dean Honywood's books and manuscripts. If you stand here and look from here at the Everest of British medieval architecture, you realize that you stand in a more worldly world. The style is of the Renaissance; the world is Charles II's. But you also understand why in homage to the achievements of the Middle Ages Wren was commissioned to rebuild St Paul's in London, making it a whole cathedral of classical majesty, a palace for the King of Kings.

Lincoln Cathedral has associations with at least two modern saints. John Wesley's childhood was spent in the Lincolnshire village of Epworth, where his father was rector. When Edward King was appointed bishop of Lincoln in 1885, he told a friend that he was glad to be going to 'John Wesley's diocese'. The statue of Bishop King in his cathedral conveys, as does the evidence about his life, an impression of powerful yet tender love, fully in the tradition of St Hugh.

21 NORWICH

In flat, windswept, peaceful Norfolk, where almost 660 churches date from before 1700, most of the main roads seem to lead to Norwich and the centre and symbol of this fine city is the basically Norman cathedral. Its spire, built about 1465 and 96 metres (315 feet) high, rises above a Close which is a village in itself, full of lawns and charming houses, some Georgian, others adapted to domesticity from the buildings of the monastery. The grave of nurse Edith Cavell, shot during the First World War, is one of the few reminders of the existence of a troubled world. From a riverside walk one looks at the boats of holiday-makers who moor here on the Wensum before or after cruising through the Broads, which are rivers and lakes made by men digging in the Middle Ages or earlier for that ancient fuel, peat.

The city became the seat of East Anglia's bishop some 30 years after the Conquest. At first the missionary bishops had clung to the coast of Suffolk, which was united with Norfolk in a single diocese until 1913. For many years the little cathedral in the Norfolk village of North Elmham had served; the battered 7th-century bishop's seat, still in use and still lifted high to face the presbytery, came from there. Then, ordered to move to a fortified town, the bishop made his headquarters in Thetford while he vainly attempted to secure control of the rich monastery of Bury St Edmunds. Bishop Herbert of Losinga, formerly a monk in Normandy, ended the uncertainty. Having reached a financial arrangement with the King (the notorious William Rufus), he began the construction of a Benedictine monastery as his cathedral in Norwich, a town which he partly demolished in order to make room. He used masons who had just finished the rebuilding of Bury. His surviving letters indicate a genuine piety and he was buried in front of the high altar; a monument now fixed to a wall may be his although it is undatable. Before his death in 1119 the work had reached from the east end to the altar of the nave, which was built by his successor with 14 bays. These two bishops created a cathedral 140 metres (461 feet) long. Its tower was completed about 1145.

The style has been called 'feminine' Norman. The east end is so spacious that there has been no need to rebuild it, so the horseshoe shape of its apse has been preserved, with chapels

radiating off the ambulatory. The nave is surprisingly light, thanks partly to the Caen stone brought over from Normandy by sea and river and partly to the Perpendicular windows which have been added to the large galleries. The decoration is plentiful and (by Norman standards) elegant.

When later generations of monks wanted to rebuild the Norman cloister the time taken, from just before 1300 to about 1430, showed that their resources did not match their ambitions, but it was their good fortune to have a superbly talented master mason, James Woderforde, in their employment in the closing stages of the work, when the bosses in the vault were completed. The cloister has two storeys (which is unique in England) and its basic system is kept throughout, but the three arched windows instructively display changing styles. The east walk has tracery which becomes more decorated in the south and west walks; then the less pointed style of the north walk is a sign of the Perpendicular period. The Prior's door from this cloister into the church is a rich example of Decorated beauty. The door which led into the chapter house survives almost as splendidly, although the house has disappeared. The nearby Prior's Lodging, built partly in the 13th century, has been extended

as the Deanery. Two gateways were built in 1316 and 1410 and have separated the Close from the city ever since.

Inside the cathedral the only major additions were of chapels until in 1362 the old spire crashed down and because of the damage a new, much taller, clerestory had to be built over the presbytery. No impressive west end was ever attempted. But Norwich and its region were becoming rich through agriculture and the cloth trade. Something of the quality of the art created locally in this time may be seen in paintings preserved in the cathedral. The best is the 'retable' now above the altar in St Luke's chapel, depicting five scenes of the sufferings and triumph of Christ. It was discovered in the 1840s forming the underside of an actual table (badly damaged, so that the head of the crucified Christ is modern) but seems to have been made for the new high altar during the restoration of the presbytery after the fall of the spire. Among the arms of prominent Norfolk families surrounding this picture are the arms of Bishop Hugh Despenser. A military man, he turned the North Elmham cathedral into a fortified hunting lodge, led a disastrous armed expedition to Flanders and savagely repressed the Peasants' Revolt of 1381. His life seems a long way from the scenes shown here.

Between the 1460s and 1510s new vaults were constructed over the nave by one bishop, over the presbytery by another and over the transepts by a third. We owe the design to the master mason, John Everard. John Harvey, the art historian who did so much to rescue medieval names from oblivion, regarded these vaults as the complete answer to generalizations about national decadence in the later Middle Ages. 'There are few more completely satisfying works than these vaults', he wrote in his *Gothic England* (1947); 'it would be difficult to discover anything more alive and articulate'.

The vaults all maintain the same star pattern with liernes and are adorned by carved and painted bosses. There are about 400 bosses in the cathedral and about the same number in the cloister, exhibiting medieval daily life or (far more frequently) the medieval imagination as it worked on the stories of the Bible.

Fortunately the bosses were far out of the reach of rioters, so-called Puritans, who smashed so much beauty at ground level in the cathedral in the 1640s. Fortunately, too, the rioters inflicted only minor damage on the monks' stalls. These were made – by the same carpenters who were indispensable in the creation of the new vaults – in the 15th century, when the pelican in latten (a brass-like metal) was brought over from Flanders. In legend this bird feeds its young from its bleeding breast. It makes a lectern where the Bible is read.

If we ask what interpretation of the Bible coming out of medieval Norwich has had most influence, fortunately the answer need not refer to Bishop Despenser. Not far away from the cathedral is St Julian's church, where a woman known to history simply as Mother Julian spent many years meditating on the meaning of visions which she had experienced on 8 May 1373, when gazing on a crucifix during a severe illness. She wrote a book, the first book by a woman in English, known as *Revelations of Divine Love*, which ended:

'I desired oftentimes to witten what was our Lord's meaning. And fifteen years after, and more, I was answered in ghostly understanding, saying thus . . . "Love was his meaning. Who showed it thee? Love. What showed He thee? Love. Wherefore showed it He? For love. Hold thee therein and thou shalt learn and know more in the same. But thou shalt never know nor learn therein other thing without end"'.

22 PETERBOROUGH

Some ancient cathedrals are at least as interesting when viewed on the outside in their surroundings as when entered. Probably not many visitors would honestly say that about Peterborough. The city is prosperous with modern commerce and industry but it has sacrificed its charm along with most of its old buildings. The cathedral's own Precincts include some historic houses but Victorian work has often replaced medieval and the monks' cloister, chapter house and dormitory have all gone. The cathedral itself lost almost all its furniture and glass to 'Puritan' vandalism and its lovely Lady chapel was turned into building material in order to pay for the main repairs. And the west front, although much photographed and praised, is not always thought beautiful. There are three pointed arches of the early 1200s, very tall and deeply recessed. Each is magnificent but the middle one, which ought to be the most important and inviting, is very oddly the narrowest. It looms over a little house in a totally different style added some 175 years later as a porch. The other arches also lack appropriate doorways and are accompanied by two modest towers. The explanation may be that two western towers were planned as the climax. If so, only one such tower was completed, about 1270. It is not connected with the gable of the façade, which itself does not correspond with the arches and does not exhibit its sculpture low enough. The other tower, lacking a top storey, is visible only from the cloister. Not everyone will agree with the enthusiasm of the Victorian historian Freeman, who called this west front 'the noblest conception of the old Greek translated into the speech of Christendom and of England'.

It is when one enters the cathedral that one is transfixed. For here is Norman architecture from end to end, begun in 1118 and complete by 1194. It retains the original central, rounded apse (although the apses of the aisles have been demolished). Like Norwich it seems light because the arcade and triforium are the same height. Helped by the clerestory, they let in any sunshine there is (through Decorated and Perpendicular windows, it must be admitted). The arcading in the aisles is intersecting, as in Norwich. But far more changing ornamentation was added than in Norwich, including the

The Norman presbytery of Peterborough.

The presbytery of Peterborough was begun about 1118. The Victorian canopy over the high altar was designed by J. L. Pearson. Above is a wooden ceiling of the 15th century.

zigzag pattern which was then a novelty, so that one feels that some Early English lightness is in the womb of the Norman stone. And again unlike Norwich, Peterborough is still vaulted in wood apart from the aisles which have early examples of rib vaulting. The ceiling of the nave has a lozenge-shaped pattern and is painted with pictures of saints, bishops and beasts as it was in the 1220s (although some areas of the paint have twice been renewed). The wooden vault of the sanctuary is more elaborate and some 200 years later. Until the 18th century the medieval *pulpitum* and wood screen remained in position. Subsequently there were other screens. Nowadays nothing

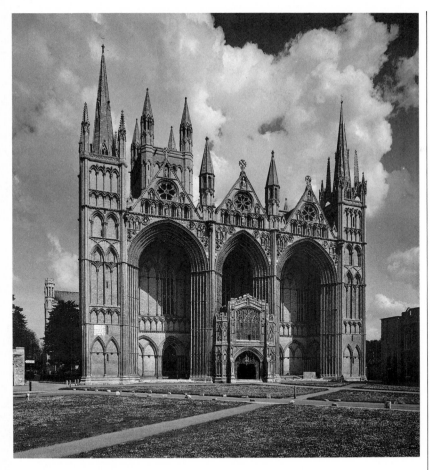

Peterborough Cathedral: the west front (mostly about 1215).

Looking up in Peterborough to a lierne vault of timber. The medieval stonework was carefully rebuilt in the 1880s, here and in the tower above.

monastery but it was refounded a century later as a Benedictine house. So it remained until in 1541 Henry VIII made it the cathedral of a new diocese, allowing the last abbot to stay on in his grand house as the first bishop.

The name 'Peterborough' derives from the enclosure of St Peter's monastery by a wall, as a fortified *burh*, about 1000. Its wealth is hinted at by the fact that under the feudal system its abbot had to assemble and equip 60 knights to serve in the king's army. To such a place the great fire of 1116 was not a lasting disaster.

The task of later centuries has been to repair this monumental church, particularly when, as Dean Patrick complained, a fortnight's visit by Parliamentary soldiers in 1643 had left 'a very chaos of desolation and confusion'. The central tower proved unsafe more than once; what we see is a rebuilding of the 1880s, using the original stone. The fine pavement, the rather less praiseworthy canopied high altar and the furniture used by choir and clergy are slightly later; they were designed by J. L. Pearson. This sanctuary has been lightened by a retrochoir built at the end of the 15th century, almost certainly by John Wastell, who went on to do a similar but larger job in fan vaulting for King's College Chapel in Cambridge. Robert Kirkton, the abbot who commissioned this 'new building' and whose initials are all over it, also started a deer park in the Precincts. But medieval Catholicism was not to last. Henry VIII's tragic first wife, Catherine of Aragon, was buried here in 1536, one of the last years of the monastery. Mary Queen of Scots followed her in 1587, until her body was promoted to Westminster Abbey. There is an 18th century copy of a portrait of the grave-digger who buried both queens, Robert Scarlett.

In theatrical Peterborough Cathedral one feels what T. S. Eliot felt in the tiny church of Little Gidding, which is not far away:

> You are here to kneel
> Where prayer has been valid. . . .
> And what the dead had no speech for, when living,
> They can tell you, being dead: the communication
> Of the dead is tongued with fire
> Beyond the language of the living.

divides the length of 146 metres (481 feet). Instead a modern rood is hung high up, a golden figure on a red cross.

Worship has been offered here since about 655, when a monastery was founded by the royal family of Mercia. It stood on the edge of the waters of the Fens but was fortunate in that it attracted many benefactions and was enabled to turn them into fine building by the proximity of the quarry of Barnack, which it owned. This stone was used until the quarry was exhausted towards the end of the Middle Ages. Special tombs – for example, of abbots (which survive in a unique series) – could use the marble-like limestone of Alwalton, only five miles away. In 870 the Danes destroyed the by now rich

23 ST ALBANS

A medieval painting in the nave of St Albans shows William Fitzherbert, Archbishop of York in the reign of Stephen.

The stone reredos above the high altar of St Albans was built in 1484 although the figures are Victorian. Behind it is the replacement of the Norman east end, started in 1257.

The long, low building of St Albans Cathedral is spectacular in one sense: it illustrates how dramatic the history of the English Church can be in triumph, in decline and, after the removal of privilege and pride, in revival.

Triumphantly St Albans houses the shrine of Britain's first Christian martyr, a soldier executed here (or hereabouts) in 209 (or thereabouts) for sheltering a priest on the run during a persecution and for admitting that he had been converted by him. What remains of Verulamium, the important Roman town where he was condemned, now lies in ruins beneath green fields. Watling Street, the backbone of the Roman road system, here crossing the river Ver, is now no rival to the adjacent M1 and A1. But on this hilltop a great church honouring St Alban has endured. There is a record of a pilgrimage in 429 by a French bishop and Bede's *Ecclesiastical History* says that 'a church of wondrous workmanship' was the scene of miracles of healing in the 720s. Some 70 years later Offa, King of Mercia, founded a monastery here and small pillars probably from the Anglo-Saxon church are still visible in the triforium running round the Norman transepts. Viking invaders are said to have stolen St Alban's bones, which were recovered by a monk who became a daring spy.

The church's triumph went from strength to strength in the Middle Ages. Abbot Paul, Archbishop Lanfranc's nephew, was brought over from Caen in Normandy to reform and rebuild the monastery. He had to rely on the flint scattered over the chalky fields and on Roman bricks from Verulamium, which he had covered externally as well as internally with whitewashed plaster. This meant that there could be almost no carving for ornamentation in the massive new church consecrated in 1115 and no great height could be risked, so that the central tower was squat although in the Middle Ages it was crowned by a spire in timber. But in 1156 the Abbot of St Albans was declared the premier abbot of the Benedictine order in England. This promotion above Glastonbury came from the only Englishman ever to be elected Pope, Nicholas Brakespeare (Adrian IV), who had been born in the town and grew up around the monastery's walls.

In 1195 Abbot John of Cella embarked on the modernization of the nave for the monks' altars and processions. It was and is England's longest nave at 84 metres (275½ feet) but he managed to rebuild four bays in the Early English style at the east end, using stone from the quarry which had been discovered in the village of Totternhoe. When five bays on the south side of the remaining Norman work collapsed 125 years later, killing two monks and a boy, they were rebuilt in the Decorated style. But about a quarter of the nave remained Norman. Why? Immediately it was probably an example of money running out. But St Albans was not a poor monastery. Since the Norman quarter never was rebuilt, it can be called an example of medieval conservation which is rare and which cannot be said to be beautiful.

Successive abbots concentrated on areas other than the nave, which never received the stone vault and the west towers once intended. A parish church was built right next door and many buildings for the monks' own use arose, some splendidly. The monastery needed about 100 servants and had stables for about 300 horses. It dominated the economy as well as the church life of the surrounding town and countryside and there were riots in protest at its wealth and power. But among the monks were some excellent artists and craftsmen. A unique series of wall and roof paintings survives in the great church and books which were 'illuminated' in the cloister are among the treasures of libraries in Oxford, Cambridge and London. There were also distinguished scholars and one man, Matthew Paris, who became a monk in 1217 excelled as a journalist as well as in the arts of sculpture, metalwork and painting. It is significant that histories produced here by Matthew Paris and his successors were called *The Deeds of the Abbots*, for the Abbot of St Albans, who dressed like a bishop, lived and ruled like a lord. Kings and noblemen found his house, 20 miles north of London, a convenient hotel. Near the high altar are the chantry or memorial chapels of two great abbots and the no less significant brass memorial of Abbot Thomas de la Mare. Their abbey also contains a memorial to a guest – the tomb of Humphrey Duke of Gloucester, brother to Henry V and Regent after his death.

Troubles came to the monastery, especially during the Black Death when all but 13 of the 60 monks died and the Wars of the Roses when

two battles were fought in the town's streets. In 1381 the abbot was temporarily forced to promise to free all the serfs (semi-slaves) on the estates. And there were financial problems; a statue of St Alban, installed near his shrine, nodded to the pilgrim only when his offering was thought adequate. But the church's triumph seemed secure. Between nave and choir a very solid (but not symmetrical) stone screen still survives although the rood above it, and the screens which extended into the aisles, have gone. Behind it the monks maintained their round of worship in full dignity. The east end of the church was extended to the window of the Lady chapel, a piece of geometry from the early 1300s, and a watching chamber in oak shows the need to guard the gold and jewels of the shrine from the early 1400s. The fine stone reredos above the high altar was built in 1484 although the figures one sees are Victorian.

The monks could not guard themselves, however, against Henry VIII or against the hatred of the townspeople released by the dissolution of the monastery in 1539. The physical results were now spectacular. The shrine was knocked into pieces (which have now been put together again). Almost all the monastic buildings were torn down apart from the gatehouse which had been built as a fortification to keep the town out and which now became the town's own gaol. The parish church provided by the monks was torn down and the great church escaped this fate only because it became the parish church, with a public footpath where the retrochoir had been and the Lady chapel turned into the town's grammar school. It proved, of course, too cold and too expensive. The once white and once sumptuous church had been left to decay almost into a complete ruin when in 1877 it was needed as a cathedral, to serve the growing population of the counties of Hertford and Bedford.

At this stage St Albans' history was dominated by a millionaire as masterful as any of its medieval abbots, Lord Grimthorpe. He became the key figure because as yet it was not possible to afford a proper staff of dean and canons. He spent a fortune on the restoration of the fabric but insisted that it should all be made to his own designs. His window in the north transept has been compared with an exhibition of Victorian coinage and his west end is not admired. The ensuing outcry led to the formation of a Society for the Protection of Ancient Monuments, led by William Morris. But the lancet windows in the south transept are better. The vandal was also the saviour.

In the 20th century this cathedral, still called 'the Abbey', has prospered and probably those who love it will make sure that its Victorian, no less than its Norman, work is conserved. It is the centre of a lively diocese and draws a large regular congregation. A new chapter house, designed by William Whitfield and opened in 1982, includes a restaurant packed by visitors. It has meeting rooms and offices where the many services and cultural and educational activities are organized. And its modern bricks deliberately echo those once brought up the hill to build a great church from the Roman empire's ruins.

24 ST PAUL'S

Significantly it is always referred to not as 'London Cathedral' but as 'St Paul's' – and that was the custom long before London had other cathedrals (the Roman Catholic cathedral of Westminster and Southwark's Anglican and Roman Catholic cathedrals). Millions of tourists go there every year from all over the world and millions of pounds have been given in recent years to repair and clean its fabric, but like Durham Cathedral it is not exactly a church one is 'fond of'. On Ludgate Hill it is a towering landmark. It proclaims the glory of the Lord; it celebrates the moral and physical strength of England and the respectable wealth of the City of London; and it does so confidently and colossally. From foundations to dome it is the masterpiece of the greatest of English architects, Sir Christopher Wren. But it is a monumental masterpiece, and it cuts ordinary human nature down to size. There is a statue of a great poet of love, John Donne, who ended up as Dean of St Paul's – but he is in his shroud, awaiting burial in 1631. There was no Lady chapel until 1959. The very modern Mother and Child by Henry Moore is elemental rather than lovely and the cherubic children who delighted earlier carvers in stone and wood are not nearly as prominent as the statues of the conquering heroes of the British empire. In Portland stone and marble, St Paul's seems to need trumpets and a great congregation. It is used best on splendid occasions of national thanksgiving led by the monarch. The music of Handel seems made for it. It is glorious. It belongs to something greater than London.

In its grandeur and its basic plan St Paul's is an echo – as clear an echo as anything to be heard in the famous Whispering Gallery around the inside of the dome. For Old St Paul's, largely destroyed in the Great Fire of 1666, was one of the largest churches in the world. In the Middle Ages, as later, the merchants of London were determined not to be outclassed by the royal church of Westminster dedicated to St Peter; Paul must be at least the equal of Peter. We know this church from a number of descriptions in words, usually excited, and from the engravings by the Czech refugee, Wenceslaus Hollar, in Dugdale's *History of St Paul's Cathedral* (1658). It was almost 183 metres (600 feet) long after extensions in the 13th century, and its spire was about 26 metres (85

feet) higher than Salisbury's. Its chief feature was the shrine of St Erkenwald, a bishop who had built a stone cathedral about 680 (although a small church, probably wooden, had been built by the first bishop among the Anglo-Saxons, Mellitus, almost 80 years before). That cathedral, damaged by the Vikings and rebuilt, had been one of the churches which burned down at a date convenient to the Normans, who had bigger ideas.

A nave of 12 bays and a choir were ready in time for the shrine to be moved behind the high altar in 1148. About 100 years later work was begun on a new choir, to house a still more magnificent shrine beneath the country's largest rose window – which, surmounting seven smaller lancet windows, was England's reply to the rose windows in the transepts of the great cathedral of Paris, Notre Dame. On the south side were the cloister and the chapter house for the numerous clergy including 30 'major' canons who were men of considerable income and 12 'minor' canons who formed their own college and were men of considerable stamina for the many services.

On the north side a famous open air pulpit, Paul's Cross, became a centre for Protestant preaching in the 16th century and once the splendid Catholic ceremonies had been

The west front and dome of St Paul's, designed by Sir Christopher Wren and built between 1675 and 1710. In front is a statue of Queen Anne.

abolished the size of Old St Paul's became purposeless. St Erkenwald was forgotten. The spire was never rebuilt after being struck by lightning. The custom of using the nave ('Paul's Walk') as a shopping centre and fashionable promenade grew in noise and scandal. When the west end needed drastic repair the solution (in 1633-42) was very drastic: the portico of a Corinthian temple was built here by Inigo Jones.

Later, Wren proposed replacing the central tower of Old St Paul's by a dome and repairing the nave and transepts in the classical style of the Renaissance. When dealing with Salisbury Cathedral or Westminster Abbey he showed much more respect for medieval architecture and it says something about the general boredom with Old St Paul's that here he wrote contemptuously about 'Gothick rudeness'.

After the Great Fire of 1666 Wren suggested the rebuilding of the whole City of London with symmetrical streets. But he cannot have thought that his hasty plan would be taken seriously and all that came of his disregard of memories and vested interests was the building of some 50 new churches and a cathedral, mostly paid for by a tax on coal entering London. Even that outcome was not certain: there was no money from insurance. The Church of England did not dominate society as the new churches were to dominate the capital's skyline; on the contrary, it had recently been persecuted by the Puritans and its supreme governor, King Charles II, was to die a Roman Catholic. And the Church resisted novelties. The Bishop of London urged 'nine considerations against building a new cathedral' and there was delay in demolishing the blackened ruins of the old.

Work on the new cathedral did not begin until 1675 because there was so much criticism of Wren's successive plans. After a first attempt which was generally and rightly condemned as dull, he produced an ambitious and beautiful model (now displayed in the crypt). It was vetoed by the clergy. Their objection was that the choir and the nave were both too short, for Wren had sacrificed all medieval traditions to his vision of a congregation being preached to under the clear light coming down from a great dome. At first he was willing to compromise with conservation only by a domed portico at the west end, with two chapels protruding sideways behind the entrance. Was the idea of the dome inspired by his memory of the octagon in Ely, where his uncle had been bishop? And was the west end also a classicized echo of Ely? It seems likely. But the shape of his dome was influenced by Lemercier's dome over the Sorbonne in Paris (which he had seen) and by Bramante's frustrated design for St Peter's in Rome (which he never visited).

The model eventually accepted as the Royal Warrant Design was not quite final. Wren was allowed 'liberty in the prosecution of his work to make variations rather ornamental than essential' and he took full advantage of that permission. The final plan had compromise written into it. There was to be a dome, of lead-sheathed timber resting on a cone of brick hidden behind the stone, and it was to weigh 64,000 tons, but it was not to end in a giant pineapple as Wren had once imagined. Nor was there to be a steeple rising in six stages, his next idea. On top of a small steeple there was to be a globe under a cross. There was to be a classical portico at the west end, but the two bell towers above it (the last part of the cathedral which Wren completed) were to be much more elaborate than in the Royal Warrant Design. There was to be a classical system in the whole church, but its shape was to be medieval and therefore cruciform. In the nave of three great bays as well as under the dome, a large congregation would be able to see the altar as well as the preacher, although thanks to Wren's insistence on symmetry the choir was also to have three bays. In the choir the clergy and singers were to be seated in stalls carved sumptuously by Grinling Gibbons and were to be separated from the nave by an iron screen made magnificently by Jean Tijou (later moved to the aisles). The outer walls were to be classical but even here classicism was to be compromised. At the top there was to be a balustrade, which Wren thought vulgar; there were to be two storeys because it proved impossible to obtain enough stones large enough to make high columns; and the walls were to be no more than screens hiding the flying buttresses which supported the separate walls and vaults of choir and nave. And there was to be a crypt as in a medieval church, although in unmedieval fashion it was to extend for the whole length of the cathedral. Wren even allowed a medieval mistake to be repeated; the piers inside the church were filled with rubble which worked loose and had to be solidified by many tons of cement in the 1930s.

Building took from 1675 to 1710. During that period William Sancroft, who as Dean of St Paul's was chiefly responsible for the administration of the crucial first phase, became Archbishop of Canterbury, protested against the actions of James II, refused to swear allegiance to William and Mary after James's overthrow, was deprived of office and died. Wren was almost 80 at the end, but he lived to see his often-revised plan realized and the famous inscription above his tomb (in Latin) is entirely right: 'If you seek his monument, look around you'. And we look at a work of genius.

Showing the quality of English art and

craftsmanship early in the 18th century, Sir James Thornhill added eight monochrome frescos illustrating the life of St Paul on the inside of the dome (although Wren wanted mosaics). Jacob Sutton created the eagle lectern and Francis Bird carved a massive font and the statues above the west end. But the next major additions had to wait until long after Wren's death. No monument was allowed in the cathedral until it was felt that a Quaker reformer of prison life, John Howard, must be honoured; he died in 1790. After that, grand memorials crowded in to celebrate the victories of the Napoleonic wars. The Duke of Wellington has an immense monument in the nave representing 20 years' work by Alfred Stevens and Nelson has a smaller but fine statue by John Flaxman. Both heroes have tombs in the crypt; Nelson's is a black marble sarcophagus originally constructed for Cardinal Wolsey. Eventually St Paul's became almost a history of the British empire in stone and the Order of the British Empire has its chapel in the crypt (with St Michael and St George in the nave). But another addition came in Victorian and Edwardian times — glittering mosaics over the choir and transepts by Sir William Richmond and the Venetian Antonio Salviati. These matched the church music which under organists such as Sir John Stainer and Sir George Martin enthralled great congregations. The spirituality of that age is reflected in the picture by William Holman Hunt (in 1900) of Christ knocking at the door as 'the Light of the World'. The expansion of the British empire was celebrated alongside the light-spreading missionary work of the Victorian Church of England.

In the sadder 20th century the impact of total war has left its mark on the cathedral. All Souls Chapel, on the left after entering at the west end, is a memorial to Lord Kitchener and other casualties of 1914-18. The high altar and the baldacchino or canopy above it commemorate the dead from the Commonwealth in 1939-45 and behind it is the American

The Whispering Gallery under the dome of St Paul's surmounts mosaics added by Sir William Richmond in the 1890s. The iron screen by Jean Tijou and the carving of the choir stalls and organ case by Grinling Gibbons are examples of craftsmanship commissioned by Wren.

Memorial Chapel — all replacing earlier work which was destroyed by bombs, as was part of the north transept. The photograph of the dome serene above the flames of an air raid in December 1940 raised morale throughout the nation and a plaque under the dome commemorates Sir Winston Churchill's funeral in 1965. The Choir School designed by Leo de Syllas is one of the few buildings in the post-war reconstruction of the city which are generally thought fit to stand beside the work of Wren.

The City of London to this day pays St Paul's a tribute in terms which prove the City's sincerity. For although the land in the 'square mile' of the financial centre is extremely valuable, tempting the construction of high-rise offices, the skyline has been kept subdued so that no nearby building is higher than Sir Christopher Wren's cathedral.

25 SALISBURY

The spire of Salisbury Cathedral, rising above the water meadows of the Avon, has been to innumerable people one of the most beautiful images of England. No wonder that an appeal for its necessary repair has met with such a ready response in the 1980s! The collection of lawns and houses in the Close, cut off from the world by a wall since 1327, is scarcely less admired. To most of us, therefore, this is a cathedral which is loved most easily when viewed from some distance. That is shown in the famous paintings by John Constable or in the exquisite engraving on glass by Laurence Whistler, one of the cathedral's modern treasures.

In comparison, the complaint is quite often made that the interior is dull. And in large measure that complaint is unanswerable – or answerable only by pointing out the colour added in recent years by much fine embroidery and supremely by Gabriel Loire's window at the east end, where the deep blue hints that it was made in Chartres. One problem is that most of the stained glass, the paint and gilding on the walls and the ornaments that added much richness to the interior have been taken away since the Middle Ages. In the 18th century the very architect who so wisely turned the graveyard into lawns, and who built proper drains for this marshy Close, James Wyatt, also persuaded the clergy to allow him to tidy up the interior ruthlessly. (Or were the clergy to blame?) In our own century the Victorian work which attempted to refurnish the choir after this devastation has itself been expelled. The 14th-century *pulpitum* was once splendidly carved and coloured. Much of it survived by being banished by Wyatt to the north-east transept, but it has never been put back in its old position – and cannot be if the cathedral is to be used as one unit on great occasions. So now everything depends on how the basic pattern in the architecture strikes us.

It is a restrained pattern. In comparison with the contemporary French cathedral of Amiens, which is 42 metres (139 feet) from floor to vault, Salisbury is only 25.5 metres (84 feet) high. The straight lines which run along the bottom and top of the triforium show unmistakably that here the emphasis is horizontal. In comparison with the nave of Lincoln (also contemporary) the vault of this

The Early English elegance of the north transept of Salisbury.

nave is unexciting and the arcade is simple; the squat triforium has only three, not six, arches to each arch below and they are matched by the three, not two, lancet windows above. There is much grey Purbeck marble blackened by the Victorians, but in the course of time most of the other stone (from the quarry of Chilmark ten miles away), originally pale buff, has itself gone grey. It is, indeed, the play of the English weather that now decides whether the impression left by the interior is to be all grey. Turner's watercolours, done rapidly as the light of a Victorian day was coming or going, recorded how the movement of such light brings life. A visit is easiest to enjoy when there is sunshine on these lawns; when there is a timeless peace, so that the sight of the cathedral's clock, still working and known to have been in the bell tower in the 1380s, causes no thought of our own more detailed watches. (Although the mechanism has no dial, this is treasured as England's oldest clock.) In such moments one can readily understand why it was in Salisbury Close that Anthony Trollope

The spire of Salisbury has stood since early in the 14th century. Its simple beauty contrasts with the more fussy west front beside the plain external wall of the cloister.

and waterless hill of Old Sarum, a mile and a quarter away, by the Normans when they moved the see from Sherborne in 1075. Although enlarged in the 1130s that church had been no more gracious than the formidable castle next door, and the decision to abandon it had been taken within the 1190s. Now that the Pope had blessed the move to a site which the Church could clearly own, free from 'oppression', a cathedral could be raised which would be in harmony with the dedication to the heavenly Assumption of the Blessed Virgin Mary.

Nicholas of Ely was the master mason for much of the time but it has been argued by experts that the chief credit for the execution of the bishop's plan ought to go to a civil servant who became one of the cathedral's own canons, Elias of Derehem. He is known to have had some responsibility for the work in Salisbury and for royal building projects elsewhere, and he supervised the making of St Thomas' shrine in Canterbury. A medieval historian, William of Malmesbury, commented not on the design but on the consistent quality of the fine jointing in the work of the stonemasons under this leadership. The new beauty was made possible by a new skill in craftsmanship, as well as a new firmness in leadership, which insisted that the canons should give a quarter of their incomes to the fabric fund. And the site was chosen sensibly, for beneath the water meadows here was a firm bed of gravel.

The new church was consecrated for worship in 1258, but the medieval will to create beauty had not yet been exhausted. Houses were built for medieval deans and canons although these have been swallowed up into the grander homes of later clergy and their tenants. And the largest cloister in England was added. The canons did not need a cloister as monks did, even if it was appreciated in the rain. Its beauty is its justification – and has been matched by the cedar trees now growing within it. It led to an octagonal chapter house modelled on Westminster Abbey's. Around the central pillar are fine carving and gloriously large windows, although the glass and floor are Victorian. One of the four original copies of Magna Carta which survive is kept here among other treasures. The line of little heads of medieval laity seems to be listening. Above these are Old Testament scenes, from Genesis and Exodus. Below them are the seats where the 52 canons, or some of them, talked. Their talk must have been to good effect, for Salisbury had a nationwide prestige. The arrangements for services on which they and their bishops agreed (the 'Sarum Use') were followed widely elsewhere. These regulations date substantially, it seems, from Richard Poore's time as dean in Old Sarum, but in the

conceived the idea of the Barchester novels and why in 1987 Edward Rutherfurd's historical novel *Sarum* (the Latin name for Salisbury, still often used) immediately became a bestseller. Here England's history rests.

This cathedral is like St Paul's in that it is a unity, largely built within 40 years. But we cannot be sure who designed it. The bishop who laid the foundation stones in 1220 was Richard Poore, a great man who ended up as Bishop of Durham (where he again sponsored dramatic building). He belonged very firmly to the medieval Establishment. The illegitimate son of a civil servant who had risen to become Bishop of Winchester, his brother Herbert had been Bishop of Salisbury before him and thanks to his brother he had become dean (1198-1215). It is probable that he was descended from a Bishop of Salisbury who had been Henry I's chief minister and the uncle – or perhaps father – of two other leading bishops. It is almost certain that what he now contributed, in addition to money, was a plan only in the sense that he insisted on an up-to-date style. He wanted a complete departure from the cathedral which had been built on the windy

new cathedral the worship reached new standards of ordered beauty.

At an uncertain date after the completion of the cathedral – perhaps in the 1320s, perhaps earlier, perhaps later – the spire was added. At 123 metres (404 feet) high, its stones had to be held together by iron bands against the pressures of the winds. At the time it seemed the peak of daring although Lincoln was to go higher and the Germans were to go higher still – in Strasbourg to 142 metres (466 feet), in Cologne to 152 metres (500 feet); ultimately in Ulm (but this was in the 19th century) to 161 metres (528 feet). There were also buildings which have disappeared since the Middle Ages – a bell tower and a couple of chantry chapels on either side of the Lady chapel (properly called the Trinity Chapel, since the whole cathedral is dedicated to Our Lady). The spire itself, weighing more than 6,400 tons, would have collapsed had great strainer arches not been added to support it in the central crossing about 1450. In later years both Wren and Gilbert Scott were called in to strengthen it. It still leans by 0.7 metre (2½ feet). But it has stood, lifting the hearts of generation after generation.

Not everything that the medieval builders created was perfect. Their west front was such a jumble of architectural motifs that Sir Nikolaus Pevsner was doing it justice when he called it 'a headache'. All but eight of the statues now in the niches are Victorian and (to make a different point) uninspired. How different this overcomplicated façade is from the east end and the transepts, where everything is neatly squared off! And how instructive is the contrast between all this fuss and the interior! If we do not complain about the 'dull' interior too quickly, we come to appreciate positively the lack of decoration in what is a work of geometry. We see the simplicity, the tall lancet windows being typical; the absence of any vulgarity; the assurance of calm faith which can afford understatement; the 'serenity, perfect poise and peace' (in the words of Dean Sydney Evans). This church which is so full of grace might almost be said to be the Blessed Virgin Mary's country house in Wiltshire.

26 WELLS

Wells Cathedral: the west front displays 293 medieval statues.

Wells and Ely are the great exceptions to the rule that a medieval cathedral must be built in a fortified town. But unlike Ely Wells had no rich monastery to explain why a bishop chose a village as his headquarters. Had such a monastery been thought essential, the bishopric of Somerset, founded in 909, might have been based on Bath, which is only 15 miles away. The diocese is still called 'Bath and Wells' and in 1088 a Norman bishop went so far as to destroy all the canons' buildings in Wells in order to establish his preference for monastic Bath. As late as 1244 a bishop was elected by the monks of Bath without reference to Wells. Or there was the possibility of Glastonbury, only six miles away. Most of the early bishops had been Glastonbury monks and in 1192 a bishop got himself appointed abbot there, in an arrangement which would have been very like Ely's had it lasted for more than 27 years. But Wells prevailed.

Some wells here were probably regarded as holy long before the little monastery dedicated to St Andrew was founded in the 8th century. Today 'St Andrew's well' is in the bishop's garden and in the cloister of the cathedral one can peer at the adjacent 'dipping place'. This sanctity was still strong in the local folk-memory at the beginning of the Middle Ages. It replaced the religious reputation which the waters of Bath had enjoyed in Roman and pre-Roman days and so Wells could offer an alternative when Somerset's bishop wished to shake himself free of the monks of Bath. It could even provide an alternative to the prestige of Glastonbury, the oldest Christian centre in England, when the monks there with their powerful friends managed to eject the bishop and keep their large revenues to themselves. But the clinching reason why Wells triumphed was that the cathedral built here was so impressive. The bishops who contributed much of their own growing wealth to the building projects, and who were the moving spirits in fund-raising, created a church which put an end to all talk of an alternative.

The cathedral which we see had predecessors – not only a Saxon church which originally may have been no larger than the one which survived in Bradford-on-Avon by being incorporated into a house, but also a sizeable Norman building consecrated in 1148.

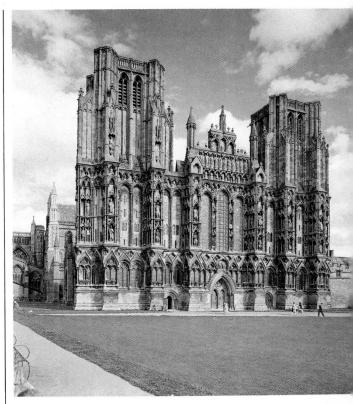

However, the present cathedral was begun by Bishop Reginald de Bohun little more than 30 years later, on a site further away from the holy wells. It was the first great church in England to use pointed arches consistently, which had not been done in the slightly earlier choir of Canterbury. It was built of limestone from the nearby village of Doulting. The transepts were added to the choir in the 1190s. Another bishop, Jocelyn, pressed on with the completion of the nave from 1206 until the consecration in 1239. He had been a canon under Bishop Reginald and the two men made sure that when Bath Abbey made its last bid for the bishopric in the 1240s the Pope could be informed that a worthy cathedral existed in Wells. How worthy it is can be appreciated all the more now that loving care in the 20th century has made it all seem fresh.

In the nave the main emphasis is horizontal. There are no shafts running from the floor to the vault, which is, indeed, not worth much attention, although some vertical emphasis is

added by making each of the piers a cluster of 24 shafts. There is a little flippancy allowed in the carving of the capitals of these piers, especially in the south transept, but any men or animals appearing there are surrounded by the 'stiff leaf' abstract interpretation of foliage. It is probable that above the high altar a reredos was erected showing Saxon bishops; seven of these figures were rescued and used as effigies on tombs when the sanctuary was remodelled in the 1320s. The whole building seems to be saying that this is Christian England, already with a long history and a moral and physical beauty, and here in Wells, as in Salisbury or Exeter, you can see that the Church is gracefully triumphant amid a prosperous countryside. The Saxons and the Normans are remembered but their struggles are over.

The next great work was the west front. Unlike the portal of a French cathedral, this was never intended as the main entrance; the north porch was that. The west front, 45 metres (147 feet) long, was built as a sculpture gallery. The projecting shafts (originally all of Blue Lias stone, but in places renewed by the Victorians in Kilkenney marble) are also unlike anything in France. They were frames for the sculptures. The master mason for the whole project was almost certainly Thomas Norreys but it is not known how he intended to complete the west front above the sculpture show. Six large buttresses suggest that he had large ambitions for towers. The present towers, added in 1384-94 and the 1430s and designed by William Wynford (who also completed the Perpendicular nave in Winchester), are probably simpler and shorter than was originally intended. Not even the sculptures could be completed before the money ran out. The apostles are from the 15th century and some niches have apparently never been filled. Another disappointment is that only traces remain of the colour with which they were all originally painted, the niches in which they stand being dark red and the walls being whitewashed. But what a work of art was created, has survived, and has been cleaned and restored, sparing no trouble or expense, in the 1980s!

There are 293 medieval statues. Two thirds of them are life-sized, those furthest from the ground being 2.7 metres (9 feet) tall. The clothing is carved with care. It is claimed that it sometimes outlines the underclothes and it is certain that a knight's armour of chain-mail is represented meticulously. The faces are all different but seem to be united by a solemn happiness. A number of carvers were at work under the supervision of one Simon. Beneath a Christ in Majesty (the medieval statue was so decayed that it was replaced by David Wynne's splendid modern Majesty in 1985) are many statues which have not been conclusively

identified because the names originally written beneath have worn away. But we can recognize a great row of figures representing resurrection themes; about 120 saints including many of the sacred heroes of the Saxons with King Solomon and the Queen of Sheba; 30 scenes from the New Testament and 16 from the Old; some 30 angels; and beautiful sculptures showing the Virgin as mother and queen. And a further excitement is suggested by the two rows of holes in the centre. It has been plausibly suggested that through them music was made by the hidden cathedral choir, so that Palm Sunday and Easter anthems announced the triumph of Christ to the waiting procession and to the graveyard.

This astonishing construction was followed by other marvels when finances recovered in the 14th century. The octagonal chapter house with many smiling faces carved above the stalls and with no fewer than 32 ribs radiating from a central pier to foliage-rich bosses was finished near the century's start. Very unusually, a staircase was needed to get to it and so a lovely one, nowadays much photographed, was provided from the east end of the church. A Lady chapel was wanted for this east end although there was already an ancient Lady chapel with Saxon origins, slightly to the south, before demolition in 1552, and so one was provided. Five great windows were placed under a domed vault with ribs like a complex star. That chapel had to be joined to the east end by more Decorated architecture of 'pure poetry' (Alec Clifton-Taylor's correct verdict). It was 'the most original treatment of architectural space of which any country at that time was capable' (Pevsner). The chancel was thought to need a

new vault and so one was made, along with a clerestory and a triforium reduced to stone-work which has some of the qualities of Perpendicular panelling. And the Golden Window has brought in light since about 1340. A central tower was wanted and a calmly noble one was built in 1313-22 only to threaten the stability of the cathedral's centre. That problem was solved by the master mason William Joy, who in the 1330s persuaded the clergy to allow him to introduce immense inverted arches in order to take the strain. These are sometimes criticized as being grossly insensitive. Undeniably they show supreme daring. But they were redeemed in the 1480s by having a rood placed over them, which made the strainer arch which faces the nave a platform for the great Christian symbol; and in 1920 another Crucifixion was put here, to great effect.

More than 50 canons were entitled to stalls and incomes in this grand cathedral from 1135 to 1592 and their 'vicars' remained as a kind of college until 1933. For these vicars 42 houses were built in the 14th century, with a dining hall, a chapel, a library and a bridge to the cathedral added later and this Vicars' Close remains as a unique medieval street. The 15th century saw the rebuilding of a large (but only three-sided) cloister with a larger library for the canons on the other side of the church. Of the stalls on which the clergy sat or leaned during services, 64 misericords survive. (The stalls are mostly Victorian but are brightened by splendid needlework done by women of the diocese in 1937-49.) But all this is eclipsed by the baronial splendour in which the bishop has been housed since the 13th century (with later additions). Inside the cathedral there can be no greater contrast between the plain Saxon font and the subtle architectural masterpieces which are now above and around it. Outside, the contrast is equally marked between the holy wells venerated by the Saxons and the moat on which swans move with an aristocratic grace around the Bishop's Palace.

Such magnificence could not last. It was crazy that so much of the wealth of medieval Somerset was applied to the upkeep of Wells and Glastonbury. A plain stone pulpit in the Renaissance style was given in 1547 by a bishop who served Henry VIII. Placed in the nave, it seems to tell the people that the Word of God could be preached more economically than the Middle Ages had imagined. The end of the church's medieval splendour was also announced by hanging the last abbot of Glastonbury.

27 WINCHESTER

The exterior of Winchester Cathedral is modest, as is suitable for the church in which were buried Izaak Walton, author of *The Compleat Angler*, in 1683, and Jane Austen in 1817. He enjoyed an early and long retirement after the storms of the Puritan Revolution, fishing in the Itchen and the Test; a window in his honour includes the motto 'Study to be quiet'. She ignored the Napoleonic wars in her novels, which, although second to none in English literature, are not mentioned on her tombstone.

The cathedral and the prosperous little city surrounding it lie in a hollow of the Hampshire countryside. The area is so well watered that the crypt is flooded for much of the year. The central tower is not high (because of the unstable ground) and has lost its spire. The smaller towers planned for the transepts were never built and the Norman work which once brought the nave to a climax at its west end has been demolished. Most of the medieval monastic buildings have also gone. The Normans pulled down two churches which lay side by side to the north of the present cathedral and which were, more than any other buildings, the heart of Anglo-Saxon England. The Old Minster disappeared in the 1090s and the New Minster, containing the tomb of Alfred the Great, suffered a similar fate 20 years later. The foundations, excavated in the 1960s, are now indicated by bricks in the grass.

Virtually all that remains of the Anglo-Saxons above the ground is a collection of bones stored in chests on the screens near the medieval high altar. Some of these bones are said to belong to the first Christian king of the West Saxons (Cynegils), baptized in 635, and some to his son Cenwalh who founded the Old Minster in 648. Some 200 years later Bishop Swithun was buried outside its west door. In 971 when his remains were transferred to a shrine within, it rained for 40 days, so that folklore has always forecast a long period of wet if there is rain on St Swithun's Day (15 July). The bones of other west-Saxon kings, who made Wessex the centre of the English rally against the heathen Danes, are reported to be in the cathedral now. That is also said about the bones of Canute, the Christian king who ruled a short-lived Scandinavian empire and died in 1035.

Winchester Cathedral: the west front (about 1360).

The Normans still treated Winchester as a political centre. The Conqueror used the Anglo-Saxon royal palace and here Domesday Book was compiled to show, manor by manor, the extent of his conquest. But this was also a centre of religion, learning and art. Bishop Ethelwold had appeared in the Old Minster at the beginning of Lent in 964 and had told the clergy that they must all leave at once, to be replaced by proper Benedictine monks; so the English tradition of the cathedral-monastery had begun. But this tradition did not sufficiently impress the Norman bishop (Walkelin) who constructed a completely new church in 14 years from 1093. The transepts survive. They look unfinished, for only the arcade was built at the end, with no gallery above it. But they display the muscular vigour, utterly without ornament, of a cathedral which was from the first extraordinarily long; the length is now 169.5 metres (556 feet). Walkelin's central tower fell in 1107. Rumour had it that the cause was the burial of the Conqueror's son and heir, William Rufus, who had met a mysterious death while hunting in the New Forest. Before a new tower was built the piers which would support it were strengthened, as may still be seen.

There was some art in this rough church and some of it is still to be seen – paintings in holy books (the Winchester Bible, enriched by at least six master-artists, is still the Cathedral Library's chief treasure), paintings on walls (superb examples may be found in the chapels of the Holy Sepulchre and the Guardian Angels), and a font of sculptured black stone

The Norman nave of Winchester was remodelled in the Perpendicular style with William Wynford as master mason in the second half of the 14th century. The modern hangings are by Thetis Blacker.

(made in Tournai and given by Bishop Henry of Blois, King Stephen's brother, in the 12th century). The shrine of St Swithun was thought to need greater dignity and a new retrochoir in the Early English style was built around it as the 1200s began. As in Canterbury, only a finely-tiled pavement now remains of the glory of the medieval shrine. But as in Canterbury, one is consoled because the decision was eventually taken to modernize the Norman nave in the new Perpendicular style. Funds were available because the Bishops of Winchester had become the richest churchmen in England, ruling a diocese which stretched from the Thames to the Solent and often running the country's administration as Chancellor, an office somewhat like the modern Prime Minister's.

The nave which we see is owed to the patronage of three bishops. Handicapped by the Black Death, William Edington rebuilt the not very impressive west front before his own death in 1366. William of Wykeham, his successor, had made his first mark as a civil servant by organizing building projects for Edward III and was also the founder and builder of Winchester College and of its Oxford twin, New College. William Waynflete, the founder of Magdalen College, Oxford, finished the remodelling. The master mason, William Wynford, was instructed to keep as much as possible of the Norman work and a comparison with Canterbury, which imposed no such restriction, is inevitable. Here the architecture is less elegant but more majestic. The lines are more horizontal because the height of the Norman arches is retained. Sadly the medieval stone *pulpitum* towards which these lines moved has gone; the dark and spiky Victorian

wooden screen is not a satisfactory substitute. But even a lover of Canterbury has to be impressed as the eye takes in the more elaborate decoration above the arches, the more complicated vaulting which springs up like a row of fountains, and the finer bosses.

The monks' worship must have been encouraged by the beauty created for their part of the great church. William of Lynwode, a Norfolk carpenter, was brought here in 1308 and spent almost two years making the 68 canopied choir stalls. There is a splendid stone screen built above the high altar in the 1480s (now with Victorian figures). Much of the presbytery was rebuilt for the monks' worship by Bishop Foxe in the early 1500s and at about the same time the Lady chapel was reconstructed and decorated with paintings of the Virgin's legendary miracles. But the bishops saw to it that they themselves were honoured nobly and most of the series of chantry chapels which commemorated them were built while they were still alive. All four bishops just mentioned have such memorials and most of another chapel is occupied by Bishop Langton's tomb. Two other chantry chapels honour bishops who were great in their days – Cardinal Henry Beaufort, of royal blood and princely power (involved in the burning of Joan of Arc, whose statue now confronts him), and Stephen Gardiner who burned Protestant martyrs under Mary I. That unhappy queen married Philip of Spain here in 1554 and the chair which she used is still on view.

Inevitably such pride brought a violent reaction both in the Reformation, when the monks' cloister was destroyed, and in 1642, when soldiers of the Parliamentary army rode in and wrought much devastation. Parliament voted that the whole building should come down but Oliver Cromwell was petitioned successfully. Fortunately the 14th century hammerbeam roof of the Pilgrims' Hall survived. Later ages have added many monuments, mainly of soldiers and clergy but including S. S. Wesley, the largest figure in the Victorian revival of church music. And when the ground became drier and subsided, and it turned out that the cathedral had not been built as solidly as its appearance had suggested, it also turned out that this was not a church dear only to bishops and monks – for it was rescued by public support. Early in our own century large buttresses had to be added to prop up the south wall of the nave and a diver, William Walker, worked for over five years underground, replacing the Norman raft of timber resting on a peat bed sinking under compression with concrete resting on hard gravel. Beneath a statue it is recorded that he saved Winchester Cathedral with his two hands.

28 WORCESTER

The great church of Worcester is a bit like a snowman melting when the weather turns warmer. It was half mad to build near the Malvern Hills a hill-like cathedral mostly in the local red sandstone. This has crumbled over the centuries, so that almost none of the exterior to be seen today is what the medieval masons left. Even inside, Worcester Cathedral gives the immediate impression that it is a Victorian church. The black and white marble in the floor, for example, was brought from Ireland and Sicily. But the building of this sandstone church was not entirely mad, for enough remained in the 19th century to call forth local pride in the medieval achievement. The result was a thorough restoration. And the success of that rescue of a decaying cathedral suggests hope that there will be a similar response to the fabric's needs which a century later have again become demanding. Perhaps the best way of saying that it is a church worth all this expensive care is to compare it with the music of Sir Edward Elgar. He was born in Worcester, often conducted at festivals here and was commemorated by a *Dream of Gerontius* window after his death in 1934.

In the old days a ford crossed the Severn at this point. The strategic position was guarded but brought violence to the cathedral and city when defences were broken. Danes coming up the river looted and burned (for the last time in 1041) and Worcester was fought over in the civil wars between Stephen and Matilda in the 12th century, between King John and the barons in the 13th, and between the King and Parliament in the 17th. Some violence has been done to peace by the main road which has swept since 1794 within a few hundred yards of the cathedral to the north-east. But the contemporary writers who describe Worcester as one large traffic accident exaggerate – and its great church, which has been much photographed from the cricket ground across the Severn, reveals much beauty and brings many rewards on closer inspection.

A reminder that the historic links of Worcester are with the Midlands is given by the fact that the pioneers who organized the Anglo-Saxon Church in this area came (about 680) from Whitby in Yorkshire. The first substantial church was built by the first of Worcester's two much-remembered saints, Bishop Oswald, in

Worcester Cathedral: a view from across the river.

the 960s, when he established a Benedictine monastery. Little more than a century later the other saint, Bishop Wulstan, pulled down this church where he had been a monk – with tears, it is reported ('we poor wretches destroy the work of saints') but certainly with the intention of rebuilding in a style to match the other Norman cathedrals. Wulstan collaborated with the Normans, impressed them as a holy and trustworthy man, and was allowed to keep his bishopric; by 1080, he was the only Englishman left among the bishops. In addition to some arches in the transepts and some walling elsewhere, his church survives in its crypt. This is large and the many pillars give it a solemn dignity, although their capitals are not carved like Canterbury's. To celebrate its 900th anniversary it has been made lovely as a quiet place for meditation. The crypt's east end was, however, largely destroyed in order to make room for the foundations of a more ambitious climax to the church.

The building programme under the Normans ended with two surviving examples of the Romanesque style – the circular chapter house of about 1110 (the first of its kind in England, although the present windows and vault are Perpendicular) and the two western

In the choir of Worcester the furniture designed by Sir George Gilbert Scott was part of the great Victorian restoration.

148

bays of the nave. Probably rebuilt in the 1170s or 1180s, the bays are a curious and clumsy example of the transition to Early English. (The arches in the arcade are slightly pointed and in each bay of the triforium the six arches, although without points, are tall, with ornamentation above them.) But at the other end of the cathedral Early English has emerged fully from the womb. In this east end designed by Master Alexander and begun in 1224 everything is simple apart from the double arcading in the triforium and some restrained carving of foliage and biblical scenes (much restored); and everything is pointed, the emphasis being made even more vertical through the plentiful use of polished Purbeck 'marble'. Here is beauty. One motive was to glorify the shrines of Oswald and of Wulstan, canonized in 1203, but a royal connection was another factor in the confidence which inspired the new work.

In 1216 the body of King John was placed near these saints, as had been his dying wish despite the fact that the monks had taken the barons' side against him. The earliest royal effigy in England was made for this tomb in Purbeck 'marble' in 1232. Pilgrims still came to the saints in large numbers, but the rebuilding of the nave in an up-to-date style was handicapped not only by the Black Death but also by some diversion of pilgrimages to Gloucester. There the tomb of the 'martyred' Edward II, while not in the category of Oswald or Wulstan, was considerably more popular than King John's. The bishops and monks of Worcester must have been tempted to acute jealousy by reports of the new architecture in Gloucester while their own new nave had to be built in the red sandstone (without any Purbeck 'marble'), Decorated in style but not spectacular except in its size.

The nave was vaulted in 1377. The difference between the north and south arcades reveals the delay in completion: to the north the foliage on the capitals is abundant, to the south the Black Death has brought about the simplification which in Gloucester took the form of the Perpendicular revolution. Another hint of financial problems is given by the absence of white stone or plaster in the vault, although the shafts of stone which rise to it from the floor lead one to expect something better.

But the main reason why the nave could not be built with complete disregard of expense was that money was needed for many other projects in the recovery from the Black Death. The mighty central tower, in two storeys and originally with a spire, had been built in 1357-74 with John Clyve as master mason – the most splendid possible answer to the devastation wrought by the plague and a stimulus to all later cathedral towers in England. The choir

where the monks worshipped, beneath this tower, was divided from the nave by a *pulpitum* (now gone) and adorned with stalls with misericords which remain. Many of the monastic buildings were reconstructed. The cloister remains, as does the spacious refectory now used by the King's School. The fortified Edgar Gate was built as the entrance to the monastery; it is still there. Finally, a north porch was added as the people's entrance in 1386; it has survived after heavy restoration. That all this work was possible is a commentary on the wool trade as well as on the profits from the pilgrimages. The bishops and the monks who shared those profits owned many estates and the sheep on them continued to grow their saleable fleeces through all the times of plague and turmoil.

The Reformation emptied the cathedral of almost all its ornaments. There had been about 25 chapels in use during monastic days. Perhaps the saddest damage was done to the chantry chapel where Prince Arthur, Henry VIII's elder brother, had been buried in 1504 after dying at the age of 15. The statues in it were so mutilated that when Queen Elizabeth I was about to visit it was thought best to plaster them over, with a patriotic painting on the plaster. In a similar mood, as the stone in the rest of the cathedral decayed, it was thought best to add coat upon coat of whitewash internally and to do very little about the problems of the exterior. A tombstone outside the monks' door has on it the Latin word *miserrimus* (most miserable). Here Thomas Morris was buried in 1748. He had grown to love the cathedral as a schoolboy and minor canon but since 1691 had been excluded from its staff because he was a loyal Jacobite. And *miserrimus* was becoming true of the whole cathedral.

It was in 1856 that the Victorian restoration began. It took some 20 years. The main architect was a local man, Abraham Perkins, but Sir George Gilbert Scott was brought in to design the new fittings, including an ornate alabaster reredos over the high altar and between choir and nave a screen which has so far not been banished. Not all the Victorian work arouses our admiration in our very different century but the great windows at the east and west ends by John Hardman of Birmingham certainly deserve it. The very large cost of this programme was met through the efforts of two members of the Worcestershire nobility, the Earl of Dudley and Lord Lyttleton. They gave and they persuaded other wealthy men to give. They both earned their white marble tombs in the Lady chapel. In the north choir aisle an unrestored part was left deliberately in order to show future generations the alternative to what these Victorians achieved.

Virgin and Child *in alabaster: a 15th-century treasure of Worcester.*

The 15th-century gateway into the choir of York.

York Minster is the largest medieval cathedral with the largest collection of medieval glass in Britain and from end to end it is now full of beauty – huge, clean, airy, sunny, with bright colour from the windows and from freshly-painted stone or wood. It is a very popular place. Not only is it one of the attractions which draw tourists to the walled city in their millions year by year. It has also been the recipient of millions of pounds in recent years as the public – and not only the local authorities and the people of Yorkshire – rallied when the central tower and the west and east ends needed to be rescued in the 1970s and when the south transept was badly damaged by the 1984 fire. Yet for all its vastness, its majesty and its popularity, the Minster is a church that is curiously simple. Some writers have dared to say that it lacks charm. That is a matter of taste. What it certainly lacks is complication, apart from the stone carving on the south and west fronts.

Beneath the ground are centuries of history, partially uncovered when in the 1970s excavations were necessary in order to strengthen the foundations of the central tower with concrete and steel. When the Romans came they established on this site, which they called Eboracum, the headquarters of the infantry which guarded Britannia against the tribes to the north and against Britons tempted to rebellion. Under the south transept is the *basilica* where Constantine, who was to become a Christian, was proclaimed emperor by his troops (then rebels themselves), in 306. A century later the Sixth Legion had gone, but its crumbling headquarters continued to be used, if only as a Saxon burial ground. We know that there had been a Bishop of Eboracum under the Romans although presumably his cathedral had been located far more humbly. We also know that King Edwin was baptized here by Bishop Paulinus in 627, probably using one of the wells to be found under the present Minster. Like many other converts, the king was influenced by his wife, already a Christian. And through all the 13 subsequent centuries York Minster has stood for the alliance of Church and State in the north of England.

A *monasterium* but never a monastery (see page 30), the Minster was a centre of religion and education in Saxon times. Indeed, its great

scholar and teacher Alcuin won such a reputation here that he was called to serve the emperor Charlemagne as the leader of the campaign to revive education in Europe. Before his death in 804 Alcuin had made the alliance of Church and State a common commitment to raising cultural standards. He would feel at home in today's York, where the Minster sponsors concerts and lectures and where a modern university flourishes. The Minster he knew, however, has entirely disappeared as a visible structure. When the Normans came it had suffered from the Vikings and its rebuilding (partly in order to accommodate Vikings who had become Christians) was not impressive in Norman eyes. The poverty of the Archbishops of York in this period is shown by the custom, observed for some 60 years before the Conquest, that they were also Bishops of Worcester.

The cathedral which Thomas of Bayeux built for himself in the 1070s and 1080s seems to have been the largest of all Norman churches, 110 metres (362 feet) long and 13.7 metres (45 feet) wide in the nave alone, with a central tower about as large at the base (if not as high) as the present one. What remained of the Roman military headquarters was used to make the walls behind the plaster in the new church. Unlike the Saxons, the Normans insisted on an east-west orientation, which meant that the Roman ground plan had to be ignored. But all that remains of this Norman church is underground in the crypts. About a century later another Norman archbishop rebuilt the choir – it seems magnificently, although since this choir has been entirely destroyed we cannot know just how Norman and Gothic features were combined. In the 1220s yet another reconstruction began, which has given us the Minster we see above ground level. It took almost exactly 250 years to complete.

Apparently there were two special motives in York. One was a desire to have a cathedral even larger than the Norman one, a desire stimulated by the size of the abbeys arising in Yorkshire. When the Cistercian movement drew monks who felt a vocation to a more austere life away from rich Benedictine abbeys such as St Mary's in York, new monasteries were built without coloured glass or sculpture and often in remote, wild places. But as famous ruins such as those of Fountains and Rievaulx testify to this day, the Cistercians could not help being the creators of prosperous agriculture and of churches which, although not ornamented, were very big. To the archbishops, canons and citizens whose pride was in York Minster, the thought that Yorkshire's cathedral might be rivalled in size was intolerable. The Cistercians went in for 'grisaille' glass in their windows, painting patterns in black on white glass with only spots of colour – so the new York Minster did the same, but the craftsmanship here was superb and has earned an enduring fame in the windows in the north transept, each 16 metres (53 feet) high, the Five Sisters of York. They contain more than 100,000 pieces of glass. At the bottom is one of the panels which survived from the Norman cathedral.

There was also competition further afield. The magnitude of Durham Cathedral, and of its bishop's wealth and power, was a spur, but in the main the York clergy had their green eyes turned towards Canterbury. They never forgot that Pope Gregory the Great had intended its archbishop to be senior to his southern colleague if he was appointed first. Centuries of self-assertion by both archbishops, with incidents of childishness and violence, passed before the north was forced to accept a degree of inferiority to the south. During this dispute, and long after it, Archbishops of York had to travel to Rome and pay out large bribes in order to secure consecration and support from the Pope.

Canterbury scored a goal by winning a martyrdom. What rival to Thomas Becket could York produce? There were two candidates, both acclaimed locally as martyred saints but neither of Becket-like fame. In 1154 Archbishop William Fitzherbert died suddenly and Archdeacon Osbert was condemned for inserting poison into the wine in the Holy Communion. A former treasurer of the Minster, Fitzherbert had been elected archbishop but enemies had appealed to Rome against the validity of his election. His friends had retaliated by setting fire to the headquarters of the enemy camp, Fountains Abbey, but he had been compelled to go into a devout retirement for seven years. And in 1405 Archbishop Richard Scrope was executed for treason against Henry IV. The tombs of both men were venerated but not to the extent of a great income. Fortunately the archbishop and canons derived large revenues from their estates. Despite large expenses (including those in Rome) a prodigious programme of modern church-building could be afforded, although not rushed.

The work was encouraged by Walter de Grey, archbishop for 40 years (1215-55), promoted because he was useful to King John but turning out to be as energetic as he was rich. Using financial help from this prelate, limestone from Tadcaster and the Early English style the Dean and Chapter created a soaring south transept, where he was buried. The north transept, built entirely out of the Minster's own funds, was finished about the time of his death. That generation decided the scale which was kept in the whole reconstruction: from the north wall to the south measured 68 metres (223 feet) and the arches in the crossing were 27.5 metres (90 feet) high. This scale also meant that the weight of stone vaulting would have imposed an impossible strain on the walls. So all the new York Minster's vaults have always been wooden, painted to look like stone, carrying good bosses but still an invitation to fire. Despite this caution about the weight of stone, the central tower collapsed in 1407. The elaborate south front of the Minster dates from the 13th century. It has a splendid rose window with glass from the 16th century, complete with Tudor roses. But outside the patterns of the stonework are usually thought to be too elaborate to be entirely successful – which is partly the fault of Victorians, who added to the richness. Disappointingly there is very little sculpture.

York Minster has never had a cloister but an octagonal chapter house was built for the 36 canons during the period 1275-90, with a wooden vault (replaced by plaster in the 1840s) and therefore not needing a central pillar. The stonework here illustrates the change within the Decorated style from geometric in the windows to curvilinear in the canopies over the niches where the canons sat. The glass illustrates the transition from the grey-looking grisaille to coloured and lifelike pictures; both styles of glass-painting are on view in alternate bands in six large windows.

In 1291 work started on the nave and the contract for glazing the great west window around and beneath the heart-shaped tracery was signed in 1338. The window was given two years before his death, by Archbishop William Melton, a prominent minister in the service of Edward II and III but also a very active diocesan bishop. He had so many business interests and so many charitable projects that a modern historian, A. Tindal Hart, has written: 'Perhaps this was his greatest achievement, that he always remained solvent'. His window, seeking thoughts higher than that, shows a row of archbishops beneath a row of apostles. There is good foliage carving in the nave, although the shields of aristocratic benefactors hanging above are more conspicuous. And York's nave has height – almost 30 metres (100 feet) – with simple, vertical lines and, in contrast to the transepts, only the ghost of a triforium. If this is

not the heart-lifter we find in Canterbury or Winchester (where the Perpendicular naves are later), there seem to be two reasons. The vault of wood looking like stone is unadventurous and the breadth of 14.5 metres (48 feet) is such that the effect of height is muted.

The Black Death did not stop the programme. The nave was vaulted in 1354, and having completed it the builders turned to the retrochoir, slightly modifying the design. This task was completed in the 1400s, with great Perpendicular windows celebrating St William and St Cuthbert on either side of where the high altar then stood – but not without some experience of strikes during the shortage of skilled masons. Henry IV's master mason, William of Colchester, was lent to York for the design of the central tower, but the work seems to have taken more than half a century. St William's College for the chantry priests was founded in 1461 and remains among the handsome houses near the Minster (although there is no Close). The *pulpitum* seems to have been completed before 1461 because the last in the row of kings is the Lancastrian Henry VI (who was removed, his present statue dating from 1810) and there are no Yorkists. The celebration of Yorkshire life, including the triumph of Edward IV of York after the Wars of the Roses, took the form of other tower-building. The two west towers, completed before the final consecration of the Minster in 1472, were more ornate than the central tower

York Minster: from the city wall across the Deanery garden.

The high altar of York, designed by Sir William Tapper in 1938, in front of the east window made by John Thornton in 1405-08.

154

and of a dignity that approached the glories of France. This west front of York now possessed a symmetry which the west front of Canterbury did not achieve until 1834. But York has never displayed many statues and therefore is usually ranked below the best of the French west ends.

It is indeed remarkable that Protestants in the 1540s did not wreck the windows. We can be especially thankful that they spared the great east window with nine lights, 24 metres (78 feet) high, and tracery in two layers. This wonder combines the Old Testament with the Book of Revelation, the beginning with the end. Its bottom row includes bearded kings and younger bishops, the most expressive portraits surviving from the English Middle Ages. It was made in three years, 1405-08, under the supervision of John Thornton who came from Coventry to be the most distinguished of a whole school of York glass painters. Together with much of the central tower it was the gift of a Bishop of Durham, Walter Skirlaw, who had been Dean of York. No less praiseworthy is the deal struck between the citizens of York and the Parliamentary army under Sir Thomas Fairfax which besieged them in 1644: if they surrendered, their churches including the Minster were to be left alone.

The 18th century brought a new floor for the nave and transepts and some good ironwork. When a madman, Jonathan Martin, burned down the choir in 1829, and when a fire started by a careless workman inflicted similar damage on the nave in 1840, the damage was made good by two brothers who were the Minster's architects, Sir Robert and Sydney Smirke. Since then a line of good architects has preserved and beautified the great building: G. E. Street, G. F. Bodley, Sir Walter Tapper, Sir Ninian Comper, Sir Charles Peers, Sir Albert Richardson, Sir Bernard Fielden, Charles Brown. It is thoroughly fitting that the exhibition in the undercroft which Fielden created in the course of his rescue work in the 1970s should exhibit not only some of the Minster's treasures but also the physical and financial support needed if the Minster as a whole is to remain standing. Here as in Winchester medieval builders underestimated the need for foundations, partly because they did not expect the more efficient modern drainage to affect the moistness of mortar and earth. But the technology and the generosity of the 20th century have saved York Minster.

FURTHER READING

A reader who wishes to explore the history of Church and State, which has left so many marks on these buildings, will be interested in the three volumes of the *Fontana History of England* covering 1066-1660 by Claire Cross (1976), M. T. Clanchy (1988) and Peter Heath (1988) or perhaps in the three volumes of my *Christian England* (republished as one paperback in 1989). There are innumerable books on the cathedrals themselves and of course I am indebted to many of them although my approach is different. I have constantly consulted *The Cathedrals of England* in two volumes by Sir Nikolaus Pevsner and Priscilla Metcalf (1985) and have found that Paul Johnson's *British Cathedrals* (1980) taught a lesson in how to make a mosaic of facts readable. Alec Clifton-Taylor's *The Cathedrals of England* and Henry Thorold's *Collins Guide to Cathedrals, Abbeys and Priories*, both published in 1986, commented on the architecture with provocatively different enthusiasms. So did the shorter books on *English Cathedrals* by Patrick Cormack (1984) and Russell Chamberlain (1987). Anthony New's *Guide to the Cathedrals of Britain* (1981) and Keith Spence's *Bell Guide to Cathedrals and Abbeys of England and Wales* (1984) were more comprehensive and more severely factual. A new series of Bell's Cathedrals Guides began to appear in 1987 and in its first two years covered Canterbury, Coventry, Durham, Lincoln, St Paul's, Wells, Westminster and York. Cecil Hewett's *English Cathedrals and Monastic Carpentry* (1985) and Charles Tracy's *English Gothic Choir Stalls* (1988) were equally expert and Louis Grodecki's *Gothic Architecture* (1986) surveyed the Middle Ages internationally. In *English Cathedrals: The Forgotten Centuries* (1980) Gerald Cobb illustrated restorations since 1530 and *Visionary Spires* edited by Sarah Crewe (1986) collected designs for post-medieval cathedrals. One of the valuable features of *Age of Chivalry*, the catalogue published for the Royal Academy of Arts exhibition in London in 1987, was its bibliography. The fact that these and many other relevant books have appeared during the 1980s demonstrates the enormous public interest now being taken in Britain's cathedrals.

Earlier books should not be forgotten. I list only a few examples of the wealth of authoritative scholarship available. John Harvey, who did so much to recover their names, compiled a biographical dictionary of *English Medieval Architects* (revised in 1987) and wrote *The Cathedrals of England and Wales* (revised in 1974) and *The Perpendicular Style* (1978) among other works. John Baker illustrated *English Stained Glass of the Medieval Period* (revised in 1978) and Jean Brody *The English Decorated Style* (1979). G. H. Cook studied *Medieval Chantries and Chantry Chapels* (1968), Kathleen Edwards *The English Secular Cathedrals in the Middle Ages* (revised in 1967) and Hubert Fenwick *Scotland's Abbeys and Cathedrals* (1978). John Fitcher's *The Construction of Gothic Cathedrals* (1961) concentrated on the vaulting and Hugh Braun's *Cathedral Architecture* (1972) on practical considerations in the designs. G. L. Remnant made *A Catalogue of Misericords in Great Britain* (1969) and L. F. Salzman's standard work on *Building in England down to 1540* was revised in 1967. In the background J. C. Dickinson's *The Later Middle Ages* (1979) was a general survey of ecclesiastical history from the Conquest to the Reformation. The four volumes by David Knowles on *The Monastic Order in England* and *The Religious Orders in England* (1940-59) were magisterial and the last was abbreviated and illustrated as *Bare Ruined Choirs* (1976). George Hersey's *High Victorian Gothic* (1972) was a good introduction to a movement in art and society and *Goths and Vandals* by Martin S. Briggs (1952) was a vigorous account of restorations. The same author concisely surveyed *Cathedral Architecture* for Pitkin Pictorials (1974).

INDEX